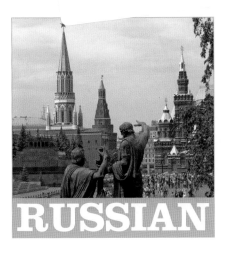

RUSSIAN

With menu decoder, survival guide and two-way dictionary

Thomas Cook
Publishing

www.thomascookpublishing.com

Survival guide.................49

Emergencies....................59

Dictionary.........................63

Quick reference................95

How to use this guide
The ten chapters in this guide are colour-coded to help you find
what you're looking for. These colours are used on the tabs of the
pages and in the contents on the previous page and above.

For quick reference, you'll find some basic expressions on the
inside front cover and essential emergency phrases on the inside
back cover. There is also a handy reference section for numbers,
measurements and clothes sizes at the back of the guide.

Front cover photography © Tim Graham/Alamy
Cover design/artwork by Jonathan Glick
Photos: Andrey (p34), BigStockPhoto.com [Elen Art (p23), Iakov Filimonov (p52),
Elena Loginova (pp33 & 35), Vladimir Tarassov (p63)], Bolshakov (p26),
Brian Jeffery Beggerly (p29), D.A.K. Photography (p14), Joongi Kim (p27),
Kecko (p7), Kok Leng Yeo (pp 37 & 41), Konstantin Ryabitsev (p17), Simon
Summers (p36), SXC.hu [Karl-Erik Bennion (p24), Lucia Pizarro Coma (p15),
Peter Suneson (p10)] and Michal Zacharzewski (p38).

Produced by The Content Works Ltd
Aston Court, Kingsmead Business Park, Frederick Place
High Wycombe, Bucks HP11 1LA
www.thecontentworks.com
Design concept: Mike Wade
Layout: Alison Rayner
Text: Marc Di Duca and Tetyana Kalinina
Editing: Paul Hines
Proofing: Monica Guy & Semen Anisimov
Picture editing: Sonia Marotta
Editorial/project management: Lisa Plumridge

Published by Thomas Cook Publishing
A division of Thomas Cook Tour Operations Limited
Company registration No: 3772199 England
The Thomas Cook Business Park, 9 Coningsby Road
Peterborough PE3 8SB, United Kingdom
Email: books@thomascook.com, Tel: +44 (0)1733 416477
www.thomascookpublishing.com

ISBN-13: 978-1-84848-104-6

First edition © 2009 Thomas Cook Publishing
Text © 2009 Thomas Cook Publishing

Project Editor: Maisie Fitzpatrick
Production/DTP: Steven Collins

Printed and bound in Italy by Printer Trento

Introduction

Russia offers the visitor an almost unimaginable array of treasures, from the cultural delights of Moscow and St Petersburg and the historical towns of the Golden Ring to the mysteries of Siberia's Lake Baikal and Kamchatka. Chief among the country's attractions is its language.

With a whole new alphabet to learn, Russian looks daunting at first, but after a little time familiarising yourself with it you'll soon be reading menus and timetables. As very few Russians speak English, this PhraseGuide will be an invaluable companion, and will aid communication from airport to restaurant table, railway station and shopping mall.

The basics

Russian belongs to the Eastern Slavic group of languages. Although these can be tricky to get to grips with, a little initial application will pay dividends. The good news is that Russian is one of the simplest in that group, and one of the easiest to pronounce.

Russian employs the Cyrillic script. There are 33 Russian Cyrillic letters, of which some also appear in the English alphabet. Learning the characters is not as difficult as it looks and will prove invaluable during any trip to the country.

Russian has a mostly phonetic alphabet, which means you say what you see. The "extra" characters in the Russian alphabet represent sounds for which English uses two letters, for example, "**ш**" ("sh" as in "she") and "**ч**" ("ch" as in "cheese"), or even four letters, for example, "**щ**" ("sh" + "ch").

The first step in your Russian language experience is to get familiar with the Cyrillic alphabet. Below you'll see the Cyrillic characters (capitals and small letters), the transliteration into English letters, and example words to illustrate how they are pronounced.

Letters		Transliteration	Pronunciation
А	а	a	as the 'a' in 'almond'
Б	б	b	as the 'b' in 'bed'
В	в	v	as the 'v' in 'vet'
Г	г	g	as the 'g' in 'got'
Д	д	d	as the 'd' in 'dog'
Е	е	ye	as the 'ye' is 'yes'
Ё	ё	yo	as the 'yo' in 'yo-yo'
Ж	ж	zh	as the 's' in 'pleasure'
З	з	z	as the 'z' in 'zoo'
И	и	i	as the 'ee' in 'meet'
Й	й	y	as the 'y' in 'yell'
К	к	k	as the 'k' in 'kill'
Л	л	l	as the 'l' in lemon
М	м	m	as the 'm' in man
Н	н	n	as the 'n' in 'never'
О	о	o	as the 'o' in 'oh'
П	п	p	as the 'p' in 'pen'
Р	р	r	rolled 'r'
С	с	s	as the 's' in 'sin'

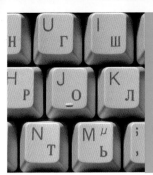

The mysterious letter ь

Unpronounceable on its own, ь softens the preceding sound. For example, "н" is pronounced as the "n" in "not". The combination "нь" is like the "ny" in the word "canyon".

Т	т	t	as the 't' in 'tell'
У	у	u	as the 'oo' in 'moon'
Ф	ф	f	as the 'f' in 'fan'
Х	х	kh	as the 'ch' in 'loch'
Ц	ц	ts	as the 'ts' in 'cats'
Ч	ч	ch	as the 'ch' in 'chat'
Ш	ш	sh	as the 'sh' in 'shell'
Щ	щ	shch .	as the 'sh ch' in 'fresh cheese'
Ъ	ъ	none	hard sign; causes an audible break in the word
Ы	ы	y	as the 'y' in 'myth'
Ь	ь	none	soft sign; 'softens' the consonant before
Э	э	e	as the 'e' in 'set'
Ю	ю	yu	as the 'you' in 'youth'
Я	я	ya	as the 'ya' in 'yam'

Grammar

This is a highly inflected language: words change according to where they fall in a sentence and their relationship with the other words around them. Inflection is governed by gender (masculine, feminine, neuter), number (singular, plural) and a grammatical aspect called case (relation to other words). Learning a Slavic language is mostly about mastering these combinations.

Russian is packed with loan words, expressions taken from other languages and transcribed into the Cyrillic alphabet. German, French, Mongolian and Turkish are common sources, and there are also many words taken directly from other languages spoken in the former Soviet Union.

Basic conversation

Hello	**Здравствуйте**	*zdrastvuytye*
Goodbye	**До свидания**	*da svidanya*
Yes	**Да**	*dah*
No	**Нет**	*nyet*
Please	**Пожалуйста**	*pazhaluysta*
Thank you	**Спасибо**	*spasiba*
You're welcome	**Не за что**	*nye za shto*
Sorry	**Извините**	*izvinitye*
Excuse me (apology)	**Извините**	*izvinitye*
Excuse me (to get attention)	**Извините, пожалуйста**	*izvinitye, pazhaluysta*
Excuse me (to get past)	**Позвольте пройти**	*pazvoltye prayti*
Do you speak English?	**Вы говорите по-английски?**	*vy gavaritye pa-angliyski?*
I don't speak Russian	**Я не говорю по-русски**	*ya nye gavaryu pa-ruski*
I speak a little Russian	**Я немного говорю по-русски**	*ya nyemnoga gavaryu pa-ruski*
What?	**Что?**	*shto?*
I understand	**Я понимаю**	*ya panimayu*
I don't understand	**Я не понимаю**	*ya nye panimayu*
Do you understand?	**Вы понимаете?**	*vy panimayetye?*
I don't know	**Я не знаю**	*ya nye znayu*
I can't	**Я не могу**	*ya nye magu*
Can you... please?	**Не могли бы вы... пожалуйста?**	*nye magli by vy... pazhaluysta?*
- speak more slowly	**- говорить помедленнее**	*- gavarich-ts pamyedleneye*
- repeat that	**- это повторить**	*- eta paftarich-ts*

Get stressed
Stress is vital in Russian. Putting the emphasis on the wrong syllable can completely change a word's meaning, or even make it nonsensical.

Greetings

Russians pride themselves on their
hospitality. On arrival, give your
hosts a confident handshake (or kiss
females on both cheeks if you've met
before). Introduce yourself using your
Christian name. If it's difficult for
Russians to pronounce, they might
assign you a Russian name that
sounds similar.

Russian speakers will be delighted
to hear a foreign guest use a few
words of their language, even if
it's just a polite *spasiba* (thank you),
pazhaluysta (please) or *da svidanya*
(goodbye) as you leave.

Meeting someone

Hello	**Здравствуйте**	_zdrastvuytye_
Hi	**Привет**	_privyet_
Good morning	**Доброе утро**	_dobraye utro_
Good afternoon	**Добрый день**	_dobry dyen_
Good evening	**Добрый вечер**	_dobry vecher_
Sir/Mr	**Господин**	_gaspadin_
Madam/Mrs	**Госпожа**	_gaspazha_
Miss	**Госпожа**	_gaspazha_
How are you?	**Как дела?**	_kak dela?_
Fine, thank you	**Хорошо, спасибо**	_kharashoh, spasiba_
And you?	**А у тебя?**	_a u tyebya?_
Very well	**Прекрасно**	_prekrasna_
Not very well	**Так себе**	_tak sebye_

Small talk

My name is...	**Меня зовут...**	_menya zavut..._
What's your name?	**Как Вас зовут?**	_kak vas zavut?_
I'm pleased to meet you	**Приятно познакомиться**	_priyatno paznakomitsa_
Where are you from?	**Откуда Вы?**	_atkuda vy?_
I am from Britain	**Я из Великобритании**	_ya iz velikabritaniyi_
Do you live here?	**Вы здесь живёте?**	_vy zdyes zhivyotye?_
This is a great...	**Это**	_eta_
- country	**- прекрасная страна**	_- prekrasnaya strana_
- town	**- прекрасный город**	_- prekrasny gorad_

A shoe-in
Make sure you wear clean and hole-free socks if you're invited to a Russian home, as you'll be expected to remove your shoes and leave them by the door.

I am staying at...	Я остановился (-лась) в...	*ya astanavilsya (-las) f...*
I'm just here for the day	Я здесь всего на один день	*ya zdyes fsyevo na adin den*
I'm in... for...	Я в... на	*ya v... na...*
- a weekend	- выходные	*- vykhadniye*
- a week	- неделю	*- nyedyelyu*
How old are you?	Сколько Вам лет?	*skolka vam lyet?*
I'm... years old	Мне... лет	*mnye...lyet*

Gifted guests

Russians think it polite to take a little something for their hosts when visiting. Wine, a cake, flowers or chocolates are all acceptable gifts.

Family

This is my...	Это...	*eta...*
- husband	- мой муж	*- moy muzh*
- wife	- моя жена	*- maya zhena*
- partner	- партнёр (партнёрша)	*- partnyor (partnyorsha)*
- boyfriend/ girlfriend	-девушка/ парень	*- dyevushka/ paren*
I have a...	У меня есть...	*u menya yest...*
- son	- сын	*- syn*
- daughter	- дочь	*- doch*
- grandson	- внук	*- vnuk*
- granddaughter	- внучка	*- vnuchka*
Do you have...	У Вас есть...	*u vas yest...*
- children?	- дети?	*- dyeti?*
- grandchildren?	- внуки?	*- vnuki?*
I don't have children	У меня нет детей	*u menya nyet dyetyey*

Are you married?	**Вы женаты (men), замужем (women)?**	*vy zhenaty, zamuzhem?*
I'm...	**Я...**	*ya...*
- single	**– неженат (не замужем)**	*- nyezhenat (nezamuzhem)*
- married	**– женат (замужем)**	*- zhenat (zamuzhem)*
- divorced	**– разведён (разведена)**	*- razvyedyon (razvyedyena)*
- widowed	**– вдовец (вдова)**	*vdovyets (vdova)*

Saying goodbye

Goodbye	**До свидания**	*da svidanya*
Good night	**Спокойной ночи**	*spakoynay nochi*
Sleep well	**Приятных снов**	*priyatnykh snov*
See you later	**До встречи**	*da vstrechi*
Have a good trip!	**Приятной поездки!**	*priyatnoy payezdki*
It was nice meeting you	**Приятно было познакомиться**	*priyatna bylo poznakomitsa*
All the best	**Всего хорошего**	*vsyevo kharosheva*
Have fun	**Приятного времяпро- вождения**	*priyatnava vremyapra- vazhdyeniya*
Good luck	**Удачи**	*udachi*
Keep in touch	**Не пропадайте**	*nye prapadaytye*
My address is...	**Мой адрес...**	*moy adres...*
What's your...	**Какой у вас...**	*kakoy u vas...*
- address?	**- адрес?**	*- adres?*
- email?	**- е-мэйл?**	*- imeyl?*
- telephone number?	**- номер телефона?**	*- nomer tyelefona?*

Shake off bad luck
When in Russia, never offer to shake someone's hand across the threshold. Doing so is said to bring bad luck.

Eating Out

Forget images of overcooked cabbage, tired pickles and tinned fish: you're likely to taste some of the most delicious food in Eastern Europe in the restaurants of Moscow and St Petersburg, as well as at kitchen tables across the land. Moreover, Russians' adoption of many dishes from their former empire has enriched the country's menus.

Most Russians only eat out in restaurants on special occasions and much prefer food prepared from ingredients they have grown or reared themselves. You are more likely to be invited to someone's home than to a restaurant.

Introduction

Russian food still suffers from an undeniably drab image, which is certainly way out of date (if it was ever true in the first place); while it may be true that, for the majority of the 20th century, the fare that most people had to queue up for was sometimes scarce and not always heart-stoppingly exciting, one does wonder if the received wisdom about Russian grub has been influenced by more than a soupçon of Cold War propaganda.

For the reality is that Russian food is tremendously varied and exciting – how could it not be, when you consider the massive heterogeneous area that the country's shifting borders have covered? What we blithely term Russian food has had a huge range of gastronomic influences. And let us also not forget that the three or four hundred years that Russia spent as one of Europe's most powerful and civilised societies – admittedly, provided that you were on the affluent end of things: they didn't have a revolution for nothing – gave plenty of time for the cultivation of a splendid national cuisine.

Today, Russian food is characterised by its heartiness, a noun that in this context is certainly no euphemism for stodginess. It's the kind of fill-your-boots fare that powers a high-octane lust for life, and you certainly won't spend your time in Russian restaurants chasing a nouvelle cuisine petit pois around the plate in the hope that it will miraculously fill you up when the other 50 per cent of the meal didn't even come close.

When it comes to the daily diet, breakfast is a quick affair and usually consists of little more than a sandwich and a cup of

Pancake day
Pancakes are one of the most popular dishes in Russia and are eaten for breakfast, lunch and dinner. They come with sweet fillings or savoury toppings.

Caviar
There's nothing more luxuriously Russian than black caviar, the roe of the Caspian sturgeon. However, most caviar you'll encounter in Russia is red and comes from salmon.

tea. Lunch was once the main meal of the day, but dinner has become the meal for which the family gathers around the table, still a very important daily social ritual. If you're sightseeing and need to stock up on some quick calories, you could do a lot worse than try a *biznes lanch* set menu.

I'd like...	Я хочу...	*ya kha__chu__...*
- a table for two	- столик на двоих	- *__stolik__ na dva__yikh__*
- a sandwich	- бутерброд	- *buter__brot__*
- a coffee	- кофе	- *__kofye__*
- a tea (with milk)	- чай (с молоком)	- *chay (smala__kom__)*

Do you have a menu in English?	У вас есть меню на английском?	*u vas yest me__nyu__ na an__gliy__skom?*
The bill, please	Счёт, пожалуйста	*shchot, pa__zha__luysta*

You may hear...

Smoking or non-smoking?	Курящий или некурящий?	*kur__ya__shy __ili__ nyekur__ya__shy?*
What are you going to have?	Что вы желаете?	*chto vy zhe__la__yetye?*

The cuisines of Russia

National specialities

Traditional Russian food very much reflects the country's rural past (and present), with ingredients most commonly sourced from its rich soils, bountiful forests and wide pastures. Flour, meat, fish and vegetable combinations are given extra flavour with berries, mushrooms and herbs. Soups of various heats and consistencies have always been a Russian speciality. Cold varieties can contain everything from fish to bread and can bring some refreshing novelty to the Western palate; hot ones are generally meat- and vegetable-based and can be amazingly – and delightfully – viscous: in some cases you might find yourself thinking if you have room for another slice as opposed to another drop!

Special mention should of course be given to *blini*, the tremendously versatile pancakes for which the recipe almost certainly dates back at least a couple of millennia. One taste and you can see why they've had a long career. They can be topped off with almost anything, from butter and jam all the way to caviar.

Signature dishes (see menu decoder for more dishes)

Пирожки	*pirashki*	Crescent-shaped, meat-filled pastries
Щи	*shchi*	Cabbage soup
Борщ	*borshch*	Beetroot and cabbage soup with meat
Блины	*bliny*	Pancakes with toppings
Котлеты	*kotlety*	Meatballs
Каша	*kasha*	Millet, oat or buckwheat porridge

The Russian bread basket

The most famous type of Russian bread is dark rye, which has a bitter taste and tough texture, while white bread and buns can have a distinctly sweet flavour.

Siberia

In the vast forests and across the steppe of Siberia, food traditionally needed to be filling and hearty to see people through the long, bitter winters. Meat and flour feature heavily in recipes, along with fish and fruits of the forest.

Signature dishes (see menu decoder for more dishes)

Пельмени	*pelmeni*	Filled ravioli-style pasta
Омуль	*omul*	Fish native to Lake Baikal
Уха	*ukha*	Fish soup

Kvas the way they like it

In the summer, *kvas* is sold out of large tanks on street corners. This popular beer-like drink is made by fermenting black or rye bread, but contains a negligible amount of alcohol.

Caucasus region

Expect a little more spice, dried fruit, mutton, cheese and rice, washed down with local wines and brandy. Many restaurants in Moscow and St Petersburg specialise in the region's tasty fare.

Signature dishes (see menu decoder for more dishes)

Шашлык	*shashlyk*	Skewered meat grilled over charcoal
Долма	*dolma*	Stuffed vine leaves
Халва	*halva*	Nut, seed or sugar paste

Georgia

The popular cuisine of this small nation is one of the tastiest and spiciest of the former Soviet republics. Fiery meat stews and excellent wines are unmissable aspects of this exotic cuisine. Russia has taken Georgian fare as its own, as the Brits have adopted curry.

Signature dishes (see menu decoder for more dishes)

Хачапури	*khacha<u>pu</u>ri*	Cheese pie or bread
Суп харчо	*sup khar<u>cho</u>*	Spicy rice and meat broth
Лаваш	*la<u>vash</u>*	Meat and veg in a bread wrap
Пахлава	*pakhla<u>va</u>*	Sweet pastries similar to baklava

Central Asia

Russia's many Central Asian autonomous regions and former Soviet Republics have a weird and wonderful cuisine all of their own. Uzbek cuisine is a spicy affair, while the Buryats of Siberia swear by steamed dumplings with a beef, mutton and pork filling. Horse meat is a staple in Kazakhstan.

Signature dishes (see menu decoder for more dishes)

Позы (буузы/манты)	*<u>po</u>zy (<u>buu</u>zy/<u>man</u>ty)*	Big meat-filled dumplings
Хойтпак	*khoit<u>pak</u>*	Fermented mare or cow's milk
Плов	*plov*	Uzbek pilau rice with lamb chunks
Бешбармак	*beshbar<u>mak</u>*	Kazakh horse meat with noodles

Zakuski
Similar to Spanish tapas, *zakuski* are little snacks to enjoy as a starter. These include many kinds of salad, pickles, caviar, smoked sausage, meat in aspic and smoked fish.

Vodka etiquette
Russian vodka consumption is an organised ritual: a designated male fills everyone's shot glass, a toast is said and it's down the hatch, with no leaving half for later.

Wine, beer & spirits

When you think of Russian drink, vodka immediately springs to mind. While there is something of a paucity of grapes in the country, there is certainly no shortage of grain, and distilling the latter as a type of wine seems to have been a logical thing to do. Vodka was probably introduced to the country by Italian merchants in the late Middle Ages and first used as a medicine – there is no doubt that it can often make you feel better, albeit briefly and sometimes with devastating side-effects! It was Stalin who gave the vodka-production industry his blessing, and while it would be ridiculously simplistic to lay the blame for the disturbance to some Russians' lives that it has caused at his feet alone, one can say that its ubiquity has caused society some serious problems.

Russia also brews excellent beers that are prompting ever greater numbers of young people to turn away from hard liquor in favour of something lighter and easier to consume by the bucket-load. Look out for the various Baltika beers available across Russia or ales from local breweries.

Перцовка	*pertsovka*	Vodka infused with chilli peppers
Коньяк	*kanyak*	Armenian brandy
Самогон	*samagon*	Homemade vodka (moonshine)

You may hear...

Что будете заказывать?	*shto budyetye zakazyvach?*	What can I get you?

Как вы это будете?	kak vy eta budyetye?	How would you like it?
Со льдом?	saldom?	With ice?
Охлаждённое или комнатной температуры?	akhlazhdyonaye ili komnatnay temperatury?	Cold or room temperature?

Snacks & refreshments

The fact that, for years, only about five per cent of Russia's population regularly ate outside the family home means that traditional snacks are surprisingly thin on the ground. However, small food kiosks appear on every busy street, purveying a variety of hot, filling food that can be enjoyed on the hop. The country embraced Western fast food virtually the moment the Iron Curtain was rent aside and the snack food market is reckoned to be growing at an annual rate of 25 per cent. There's good news for those who like a bit of froth: recently coffee shops have started to spring up in Russia's cities.

Гамбургер	gamburger	Hamburger
Квас	kvas	Fermented bread drink
Кисель	kisel	Thickened berry drink

Fast food, Soviet style
Outside big cities you may come across a type of cheap canteen called a *stolovaya*. Expect stern dinner ladies in Spartan surroundings.

Морс	mors	Forest berry juice
Чебурек	cheburek	Fried meat turnover
Семечки	semyechki	Roasted seeds (usually sunflower or pumpkin)
Таранка	taranka	Dried fish

Hidden meat
Meat-free dishes on Russian restaurant menus are aimed more at diners on special diets than vegetarians, so watch out for hidden animal bits.

Vegetarians & special requirements

I'm vegetarian	Я вегетарианец (вегетарианка)	ya vegetarianyec (vegetarianka)
I don't eat...	Я не ем...	ya nye yem
- meat	- мясо	- myasa
- fish	- рыбу	- rybu
Could you cook something without meat in it?	Вы бы не могли приготовить что-нибудь без мяса?	vy by nye magli prigatovich-ts shto-nibuch-ts bez myasa?
What's in this?	Что это?	shto eta?
I'm allergic to...	У меня аллергия на...	u menya alergiya na...

Children

Are children welcome?	Можно с детьми?	mozhna sdyetmi?
Do you have a children's menu?	У Вас есть меню для детей?	u vas yest menyu dlya dyetyey?
What dishes are good for children?	Какие блюда подойдут для детей?	kakiye blyuda padaydut dlya dyetyey?

Menu decoder

Essentials

Breakfast	**Завтрак**	_za_ftrak
Lunch	**Обед**	a_byed_
Dinner	**Ужин**	_uzhin_
Cover charge	**Платный вход**	_plat_ny fkhod
Vat included	**Включая НДС**	fklyu_cha_ya en-de-es (NDS)
Service included	**Доплата за обслуживание включена**	da_plat_a za ab_sluzhi_vaniye fklyuche_na_
Credit cards (not) accepted	**Оплата кредитными карточками (не) принимается**	a_plat_a kre_dit_nymi _kart_ochkami (nye) prini_ma_yetsa
First course	**Первое блюдо**	_pyer_voye _blyu_da
Second course	**Второе блюдо**	fta_ro_ye _blyu_da
Dessert	**Десерт**	de_sert_
Dish of the day	**Блюдо дня**	_blyu_da dnya
Local speciality	**Национальное блюдо**	natsia_nal_noye _blyu_da
House specials	**Фирменное блюдо ресторана**	_fir_menoye _blyu_da resto_ra_na
Set menu	**Комплексное меню**	kom_plek_snoye me_nyu_
A la carte	**Блюда на заказ**	_blyu_da na za_kaz_
Tourist menu	**Меню для туристов**	me_nyu_ dlya tu_rist_af
Wine list	**Карта вин**	_kart_a vin
Drinks menu	**Напитки**	na_pit_ki
Snack menu	**Лёгкие закуски**	_lyoh_kiye za_kus_ki

Tips on tipping

Waiters welcome tips. Either round the bill up to the nearest ten roubles, or leave ten per cent of the total if you're feeling generous.

Festival food

Half the fun of a Russian knees-up is preparing the feast to cover the table. Salads dowsed in mayonnaise, myriad pickles and the inevitable caviar sandwiches don't make themselves!

Methods of preparation

English	Russian	Pronunciation
Baked	Печёный	pechyony
Boiled	Варёный	varyony
Braised	Тушёный	tushyony
Breaded	В тесте	ftyestye
Deep-fried	Жареный во фритюре	zhareny va frityurye
Fresh	Свежий	svyezhy
Fried	Жареный	zhareny
Frozen	Замороженный	zamarozheny
Grilled/broiled	Приготовленный на гриле	prigatovlyeny na grilye
Marinated	Маринованый	marinovany
Mashed	Пюре	pyureh
Poached	Варёный	varyony
Raw	Сырой	syroy
Roasted	Запечённый	zapechyony
Salty	Солёный	salyony
Sautéed	Соте	sateh
Smoked	Копчёный	kapchony
Spicy (flavour)	Ароматный	aramatny
Spicy (hot)	Острый	ostry
Steamed	Приготовленный на пару	prigatovlyeny na paru
Stewed	Тушёный	tushyony
Stuffed	С начинкой	snachinkoy
Sweet	Сладкий	sladky

Rare	**С кровью**	_skrovyu_
Medium	**Средне-**	_srednye-_
	прожаренное	_prozharenoye_
Well done	**Полностью**	_polnastyu_
	прожаренное	_prozharenoye_

Common food items

Beef	**Говядина**	_gavyadina_
Chicken	**Курица**	_kuritsa_
Turkey	**Индейка**	_indyeyka_
Lamb	**Баранина**	_baranina_
Pork	**Свинина**	_svinina_
Fish	**Рыба**	_ryba_
Seafood	**Морепродукты**	_moryepradukty_
Tuna	**Тунец**	_tunyets_
Beans	**Фасоль**	_fasol_
Cheese	**Сыр**	_syr_
Eggs	**Яйца**	_yaytsa_
Lentils	**Чечевица**	_chechevitsa_
Pasta/noodles	**Макароны/**	_makarony/_
	вермишель	_vermishel_
Rice	**Рис**	_ris_
Aubergine	**Баклажан**	_baklazhan_
Cabbage	**Капуста**	_kapusta_
Carrots	**Морковь**	_markov_
Cucumber	**Огурец**	_aguryets_
Garlic	**Чеснок**	_chesnok_
Mushrooms	**Грибы**	_griby_
Olives	**Оливки**	_alivki_
Onion	**Лук**	_luk_
Potato	**Картофель**	_kartofel_
Red/green pepper	**Красный/зелёный**	_krasny/zelyony_
	перец	_perets_

Penned in
In Russia's remote provinces you may find café menus hand-written in Cyrillic script. Don't worry – the waiters will help.

Tomato	**Помидоры**	*pamidory*
Vegetables	**Овощи**	*ovashchi*
Bread	**Хлеб**	*khlyeb*
Oil	**Растительное масло**	*rastitelnaye masla*
Pepper	**Перец**	*perets*
Salt	**Соль**	*sol*
Vinegar	**Уксус**	*uksus*
Cake	**Торт**	*tort*
Cereal	**Хлопья (к завтраку)**	*khlopya (kzaftraku)*
Cream	**Сливки**	*slivki*
Fruit	**Фрукты**	*frukty*
Ice cream	**Мороженное**	*marozhenaye*
Milk	**Молоко**	*malako*
Tart	**Открытый пирог с фруктами**	*atkrity pirog sfruktami*

Tea time

Anytime is tea time across this vast land. It's usually drunk black with lemon and sugar, accompanied by cheese, chocolate or cake.

Popular sauces

Томатный соус	*tamatny sous*	Tomato sauce
Чесночный соус	*chesnochny sous*	Garlic sauce
Грибной соус	*gribnoy sous*	Mushroom sauce

Starters

Язык заливной	*yazyk zalivnoy*	Beef tongue in jelly
Икра кабачковая	*ikra kabachkovaya*	Stewed spicy courgette paste
Мясо ассорти	*myasa asarti*	Meat platter
Помидоры, фаршированные грибами	*pamidory farshirovaniye gribami*	Tomatoes stuffed with mushrooms
Красная икра	*krasnaya ikra*	Red caviar

Second course dishes

Запеканки	*zapyekanki*	Baked dishes
Каши	*kashi*	Porridge or mash
Овощные блюда	*avashchniye blyuda*	Vegetable dishes
Мясные блюда	*myasniye blyuda*	Meat dishes
Рыбные блюда	*rybniye blyuda*	Fish dishes

Side dishes

Картофельное пюре	*kartofelnaye pureh*	Mashed potato
Картофель жареный	*kartofel zhareny*	Chips, fries
Рис	*ris*	Rice
Каша гречневая	*kasha grechnyevaya*	Buckwheat
Салат овощной	*salat avashnoy*	Salad

Desserts

Мороженое	*marozhenaye*	Ice cream
Желе	*zhelye*	Jelly
Фруктовый салат	*frukhtovy salat*	Fruit salad
Пирожное	*pirozhnaye*	Pastries
Торт	*tort*	Cake, gateau

Drinks

Кофе	*kofye*	Coffee
Чай	*chay*	Tea
Какао	*kakao*	Cocoa
Морс	*mors*	Berry drink
Компот	*kampot*	Compote
Кисель	*kisel*	Thickened berry drink
Молочный коктейль	*malochny kaktyel*	Milkshake

Shopping

The bad old days of queueing up for a jar of pickles are gone; times have changed, and now Russia's cities are bursting with choice. Even customer service has improved (slightly). Things have also improved on the souvenir front, with dedicated gift shops, stalls and markets sprouting around tourist attractions. Mementos of your trip could be colourful handicrafts or the famous Russian doll.

One caveat amid all the joyful raising of credit limits: be careful what you buy as forgeries abound. Make sure that *gzhel samovar* wasn't made in China or that your new designer handbag isn't a fake.

Essentials

Where can I buy...?	Где можно купить...?	gdye _mozhna kupit...?_
I'd like to buy...	Я хотел(-ла) бы купить...	ya khat_yel_ (-la) by kup_it..._
Do you have...?	У вас есть...?	u vas yest...?
Do you sell...?	Вы продаёте...?	vy praday_otye...?_
I'd like this	Дайте мне это	_day_tye mnye eta
I'd prefer...	Мне больше нравится...	mnye _bolshe nra_vitsa...
Could you show me...?	Не могли бы вы показать...?	nye mag_li by_ vy paka_zach...?_
I'm just looking, thanks	Я просто смотрю, спасибо	ya _prosta_ smat_ryu,_ spa_si_ba
How much is it?	Сколько это стоит?	_skol_ka _eta stoyit?_
Could you write down the price?	Не могли бы вы написать цену?	nye mag_li_ by vy na_pisat tse_nu?
Do you have any items on sale?	У вас есть что-нибудь на распродаже?	u vas yest shto-ni_but_ na raspra_dazh_ye?
Could I have a discount?	Вы можете мне сделать скидку?	vy _mozhe_tye mnye sd_ye_lach-ts _skid_ku?
Nothing else, thanks	Больше ничего, спасибо	_bolshe ni_chevo, spa_si_ba
Do you accept credit cards?	Вы принимаете кредитные карточки?	vy prini_may_etye kre_dit_niye _kartochky?_
It's a present: could I have it wrapped, please?	Это подарок: не могли бы вы это завернуть, пожалуйста?	_eta pad_arak: nye mag_li_ by vy _eta_ zaver_nut, pazha_luysta?

All dolled up

Russia's most popular souvenir is the Russian _matryoshka_, a series of wooden dolls that fit inside each other. Some are delicate works of art.

Could you post it to...?	Не могли бы вы это послать в...?	nye magli by vy eta paslach-ts v...?
Can I exchange it?	Можно это обменять?	Mozhna eta abmenyach?
I'd like to return this	Я бы хотел (-ла) это вернуть	ya by khatyel (-la) eta vernut
I'd like a refund	Не могли бы вы мне вернуть деньги	nye magli by vy mnye vyernut dyengi

Moscow's Izmaylovo market

At the capital's weekend Izmaylovo market you'll find a vast selection of handicrafts, bric-à-brac, *matryoshki*, carpets, and regional and ethnic craft items.

Local specialities

These days, Moscow rivals any other major city as a shopping destination. The city is all about high-end fashion, exclusive emporia and the best choice of traditional souvenirs in the country. St Petersburg has a mixed bag of shopping options, while Siberia boasts traditional handicrafts made from local wood and birch bark. In Central Asia and the Russian Far East you'll find items with an exotic oriental flavour as well as beautiful ethnic crafts products.

| Can you recommend a shop selling local specialities? | Не могли бы вы порекомендовать магазин сувениров? | nye magli by vy parekamendavat magazin suveniraf? |
| What are the local specialities? | Что относится к местным сувенирам? | shto atnositsa k myestnym suveniram? |

What should I buy from here?	Что вы посоветуете у вас купить?	shto vy pasavyetuyetye u vas kupit?
Is this good quality?	Это хорошего качества?	eta kharosheva kachestva?
Do you make this yourself?	Вы это делаете сами?	vy eta dyelayetye sami?
Is it handmade?	Это ручная работа?	eta ruchnaya rabota?
Do you make it to measure?	Вы это делаете на заказ?	vy eta dyelayetye na zakaz?
Can I order one?	Я бы хотел это заказать?	ya by khatyel eta zakazat?

Popular things to buy

Vodka, *matryoshka* dolls, black caviar, Soviet paraphernalia, lacquered boxes, propaganda posters, Gzhel ceramics, rabbit fur hats, chocolates and bootlegged CDs and DVDs – this is the official 'top ten' of items that weigh down tourists' suitcases on their way out of Russia.

By far the most popular of these is the well-known *matryoshka* 'nesting doll', which these days are manufactured in the image of such icons as Elvis, Madonna and Barack Obama and make fabulously kitschy gifts.

Buying souvenirs

Outside of St Petersburg and Moscow, souvenirs may seem thin on the ground. The best places to look are the foyers of large hotels, local markets, outdoor museums and railway stations.

The Arbat
Moscow's Arbat Street is
the place for city centre
souvenir shops. Outside
stalls line the middle of the
pedestrian thoroughfare,
proffering anything from
Red Army uniforms to
19th-century antiques.

Gzhel ceramics also make great presents (see page 35).
The town which gives the pottery its name is about 60 km
outside Moscow and has been churning out the distinctive
blue-and-white product for over two centuries. Items can
range from clunky figurines to the finest, most delicate
porcelain.

When it comes to Soviet paraphernalia, you're going to have
to be prepared to pay top rouble for the real deal (and, even
then, do be sure to get items authenticated). Similar caveats
should apply to black caviar. Any for sale in all but the most
prestigious stores is probably fake.

Балалайка	*balalayka*	balalaika
Водка	*vodka*	vodka
Гжель	*Gzhel*	Blue and white pottery
Деревянные игрушки	*dyerevyaniye igrushki*	Wooden toys
Иконы	*ikony*	Religious icons
Икра	*ikra*	Caviar
Матрёшка	*matrioshka*	Wooden nesting dolls
Оренбургский пуховый платок	*orenburgski pukhovy platok*	Orenburg lace
Палех	*palekh*	Brightly decorated lacquerwork boxes
Писанки	*pisanki*	Brightly painted eggs
Уральские самоцветы	*uralskiye samotsvyety*	Ural minerals

| Ушанка | *ushanka* | Rabbit fur hat which covers ears |
| Хохлома | *khakhlama* | Lacquered boxes or cups |

Clothes & shoes

Moscow is by far the best place for a spot of clothes shopping, though prices are high. The city centre is awash with upmarket fashion houses and exclusive boutiques, while out-of-town malls serve the masses. However, bargains are rare, and much of what you find in Russia is probably available back home for half the price. Having said that, the further away from big towns and cities you wander, the more likely you are to come across some unique clothing that you can snap up and amaze your friends with back home. The traditional red women's costumes can be quite stunning, and, of course, no one will believe you've been to Russia unless you come home wearing a fur hat.

Where is the... department?	Где находится... отдел?	*gdye nakhoditsa... otdyel?*
- clothes	- одежды	- *adyezhdy*
- shoe	- обувной	- *obuvny*
- women's	- женский	- *zhensky*
- men's	- мужской	- *muzhskoy*
- children's	- детский	- *dyetsky*
Which floor is the...?	На каком этаже...?	*na kakom etazheh...?*

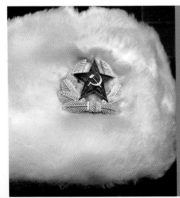

Hammer & sickle

Russia's Red Army and erstwhile Communist Party are now a source of quirky souvenirs and curios. Is a life without a chunky tank driver's watch on your wrist any kind of life?

Khokhloma style

Khokhloma is a style of painting red, gold and sometimes green designs onto a black background and is most commonly applied to wooden cups, bowls, boxes and spoons. These make excellent gifts.

I'm looking for...	Я ищу...	*ya ishchu...*
- a skirt	- юбку	*- yubku*
- trousers	- брюки	*- bryuki*
- a top	- блузу	*- bluzu*
- a jacket	- пиджак	*- pidzhak*
- a T-shirt	- футболку	*- futbolku*
- jeans	- джинсы	*- jinsy*
- shoes	- обувь	*- obuf*
- underwear	- нижнее белье	*- nizhnyeye belyo*

Can I try it on?	Можно это примерить?	*mozhna eta primyerit?*
What size is it?	Какой это размер?	*kakoy eta razmyer?*
My size is...	Мой размер...	*moy razmyer...*
- small	- маленький	*- malenky*
- medium	- средний	*- sredny*
- large	- большой	*- balshoy*

(see clothes size converter on p96 for full range of sizes)

Do you have this in my size?	У вас есть это моего размера?	*u vas yest eta mayevo razmyera?*
Where is the changing room?	Где примерочная?	*gdye primyerachnaya?*
It doesn't fit	Это не подходит по размеру	*eta nye padkhodit po razmyeru*
It doesn't suit me	Мне это не идет	*mne eta nye idiot*

Do you have a... size?	У вас есть на размер...	*u vas yest na razmyer...*
- bigger	- больше?	*- bolshe?*
- smaller	- меньше?	*- menshe?*

By GUM!
GUM department store on Moscow's Red Square houses exclusive outlets for Russia's petrodollar elite. Even if you can't afford to buy anything, you can still admire the building's grand architecture.

Do you have it/ them in...	У вас есть это...	u vas yest eta...
- black?	- черного цвета?	- _chorna_va _tsvye_ta?
- white?	- белого цвета?	- _bye_lava _tsvye_ta?
- blue?	- голубого цвета?	- galu_bo_va _tsvye_ta?
- green?	- зеленого цвета?	- ze_lyo_nava _tsvye_ta?
- red?	- красного цвета?	- _kras_nava _tsvye_ta?
Are they made of leather?	Это сделано из кожи?	eta _sdye_lana iz _ko_zhi?
I'm going to leave it/them	Я не буду это/их брать	ya nye _bu_du eta/yikh brat
I'll take it/them	Я это/их возьму	ya eta/yikh vaz_mu

You may hear...

Чем могу помочь?	chem ma_gu pa_moch_?	Can I help you?
Вас кто-то обслуживает?	vas k_to_ta ab_slu_zhivayet?	Have you been served?
Какой размер?	ka_koy_ raz_myer_?	What size?
У нас таких нет	u nas takikh nyet	We don't have any
Вот, возьмите	vot, vaz_mi_tye	Here you are
Что-нибудь ещё?	chto-ni_but_ ye_sho_?	Anything else?
Вам это завернуть?	vam eta zaver_nut_?	Shall I wrap it for you?
Это стоит (пятьдесят рублей)	eta _sto_yit pyatde_syat_ rub_ley_	It's (50 roubles)
Это со скидкой	eta sa_skid_kay	It's reduced

Where to shop

Where can I find a...	Где находится...	gdye na_kho_ditsa...
- bookshop?	- книжный магазин?	- _knizhny_ maga_zin_?
- clothes shop?	- магазин одежды?	- maga_zin_ o_dyezhdy_?
- department store?	- универмаг?	- univer_mag_?
- souvenir/gift shop?	- сувенирный магазин?	- suve_nirny_ maga_zin_?
- music shop?	- магазин музыкальных инструментов?	- maga_zin_ muzi_kal_nykh instru_men_taf?
- market?	- базар?	- ba_zar_?
- newsagent?	- газетный киоск?	- ga_zetny_ ki_osk_?
- shoe shop?	- обувный магазин?	- _obuvny_ maga_zin_?
- stationer's?	- канцтовары?	- kantsta_vary_?
- tobacconist?	- магазин табачных изделий?	- maga_zin_ ta_bach_nykh iz_dyely_?

Where's the best place to buy...?	Где лучше всего купить...?	gdye _lucheh_ fsye_vo_ ku_pit_...?
- a film	- плёнку	- _plyonku_
- an English newspaper	- газету на английском	- ga_zetu_ na an_gliskom_
- a map	- карту	- _kartu_
- postcards	- открытки	- at_kritku_
- a present	- подарок	- pa_darak_
- stamps	- марки	- _marki_
- sun cream	- солнцезащитный крем	- sontseza_shchitny_ krem

Gzhel ceramics

The village of Gzhel has been known for its pottery since the 14th century. The widely available swirling blue-and-white folk design is applied to myriad kitchen items.

Food & markets

Is there a supermarket/ market nearby?	Здесь есть поблизости супермаркет/ базар?	zdyes yest pablizasti supermarket/ bazar?
Can I have...	Дайте пожалуйста...	daytye pazhaluysta...
- some bread?	- хлеб	- khlyeb
- some fruit?	- фрукты	- frukty
- some cheese?	- сыр	- syr
- a bottle of water?	- бутылку воды	- butylku vady
- a bottle of wine?	- бутылку вина	- butylku vinah
I'd like... of that	Дайте пожалуйста...	daytye pazhaluysta...
- half a kilo	- полкило	- polkiloh
- 250 grams	- двести пятьдесят грамм	- dvyestye pyatdesyat gram
- a small/big piece	- небольшой/ большой кусок	- nyebalshoy/ balshoy kusok

Import & export

You cannot legally take out of the country anything that's more than a hundred years old. Items produced before 1975 must be given the all clear by the Ministry of Culture before you can export them. It's officially illegal to take roubles out of the country.

St Petersburg's Nevsky prospekt

The best central shopping area in Russia could well be St Petersburg's Nevsky prospekt, the main thoroughfare that cuts the city centre in two. It has everything from souvenir stalls to high-end fashion and department stores.

ПЕКИН —— УЛАН-БАТОР —— МОСКВА
北京 —— 乌兰巴托 —— 莫斯科
БЭЭЖИН —— УЛААН-БААТАР —— МОСКВА

Getting Around

In such a vast country, an efficient
transport system is essential. Moscow
has buses, a few trams and a famous
metro system, the busiest in the world.
Flights are limited and most long
distance journeys between cities are made
by sleeper train. Buses and minibuses
take over in urban areas and between
smaller towns and villages. Out in the
sticks expect perhaps only one bus a
day. Thankfully, the whole system is
cheap and easy to use.

Few choose to hire a car in Russia,
and for good reason. Road surfaces
are horrendous, driving standards
low and accidents not infrequent.
Moscow is gridlocked for most of the
day, and St Petersburg is little better.

Arrival

Airport passport checks and customs are unintrusive and over swiftly, and you'll be in the arrivals lounge before you know it. All of Russia's airports are connected to the city centre by public transport – don't let unofficial taxi touts convince you otherwise.

Where is/are the...	Где...	gdye...
- luggage from flight...?	- багаж с самолёта...?	- ba_gazh_ sama_lyo_ta...?
- luggage trolleys?	- багажная тележка?	- ba_gazh_naya tye_lesh_ka?
- lost luggage office?	- бюро потерянного багажа?	- byu_ro_ pat_ye_ryanava baga_zha_?

Where is/are the...	Где...	gdye...
- buses?	- автобусы?	- av_to_bus?
- trains?	- поезда?	- payez_da_?
- taxis?	- такси?	- tak_si_?
- car rental?	- машины напрокат?	- ma_shiny_ napra_kat_?
- exit?	- выход?	- _vy_khad?

How do I get to hotel...?	Как проехать до гостиницы...?	kak pra_ye_khach-ts da gast_i_nitsy...?

My baggage is...	Мой багаж...	moy ba_gazh_...
- lost	- потерян	- pat_ye_ryan
- damaged	- повреждён	- pavrezh_dyon_
- stolen	- украден	- u_kra_dyen

The *marshrutka*

A *marshrutka* minibus is a fixed-route taxi charging a flat-rate fare through Russia's cities. They're much faster than other types of bus but are slightly more expensive.

Romance of the Russian rails

A train journey is a quintessential Russian experience. There's nothing more romantic than watching the snowbound countryside slide past your carriage window.

Customs

To enter Russia most foreigners need a visa, which should be obtained at least a month before travelling. If your papers are in order, passport checks are painless and over quickly, but don't expect too many smiles.

The children are on this passport	**Дети записаны в этом паспорте**	_dyeti zapisany v etam paspartye_
We're here on holiday	**Мы в отпуске**	_my fotpuskye_
I'm going to...	**Я еду в...**	_ya yedu f..._
I have nothing to declare	**Мне нечего декларировать**	_mnye nyechevo deklarirovat_
Do I have to declare this?	**Это нужно декларировать?**	_eta nuzhna deklarirovat?_

Car hire

Unless you've experienced motoring in the world's driving black spots, forget car hire in Russia. Without thorough knowledge of the unwritten rules of the Russian roads, you'll be putting yourself and your passengers at considerable risk. Take the train.

I'd like to hire a...	**Я бы хотел (-ла) взять напрокат...**	_ya by khatyel (-la) vzyat naprakat..._
- car	**-машину**	_- mashinu_
- people carrier	**-микроавтобус**	_- mikra'avtobus_
with...	**с...**	_s..._
- air conditioning	**- кондиционером**	_- kanditsionyerom_
- automatic transmission	**- автоматической коробкой передач**	_- avtamaticheskoy karobkay peredach_

How much is that for a...	Сколько стоит в...	skolka stoyit v...
- day?	- день?	- den?
- week?	- неделю?	- nyedyelyu?

Does that include...	Это включая...	eta fklyuchaya...
- mileage?	- километраж?	- kilametrazh?
- insurance?	- страховку?	- strakhovku?

On the road

Driving on Russia's city streets and country highways is not for the fainthearted. Suicidal overtaking, erratic and aggressive driving style, drunks behind the wheel and constant police checkpoints make for an unpleasant motoring experience. Most people would never dream of driving through the city, never mind going out on the open road.

What is the speed limit?	Какое ограничение скорости?	kakoye agranichenye skorasti?
Can I park here?	Здесь можно запарковаться?	zdyes mozhna zaparkavatsa?
Where is a petrol station?	Где находится бензоколонка?	gdye nakhoditsa benzakalonka?

Please fill up the tank with...	Пожалуйста залейте в бак...	pazhaluysta zaleytye v bak...
- unleaded	- очищенного бензина	- achishchenava benzina
- diesel	- дизтоплива	- diztopliva
- leaded	- неочищенного	- nyeachishchenava
- LPG	- газолина	- gazolina

Directions

Is this the road to...?	Это дорога на...?	eta daroga na...?
How do I get to...?	Как мне доехать до...?	kak mnye dayekhach-ts da...?
How far is it to...?	Как далеко до...?	kak daleko da...?
How long will it take to...?	За сколько я доеду до...?	za skolka ya dayedu da...?
Could you point it out on the map?	Можете мне показать это место на карте?	mozhetye mnye pakazach-ts eta myesta na kartye?
I've lost my way	Я заблудился	ya zabludilsya

Slava/sprava

English	Russian	Pronunciation
On the right/left	Слева/справа	sleva/sprava
Turn right/left	Поверните направо/налево	pavyernitye naprava/naleva
Straight ahead	Прямо	pryama
Turn around	Развернитесь	razvyernityes

Public transport

Russia's public transport system is in relatively good shape, especially in Moscow and St Petersburg where the metro will take you anywhere you want to go quickly, punctually and for just a few roubles. Tickets for many trams and buses can be bought from ticket windows and news kiosks in advance, or from the conductor on board.

English	Russian	Pronunciation
Bus	Автобус	avtobus
Bus station	Автостанция	avtostantsiya
Train	Поезд	poyezd
Train station	Железнодорожный вокзал	zheleznadarozhny vagzal
I would like to go to...	Я еду в...	ya yedu f...
I would like a... ticket	Мне билет...	mnye bilyet...
- single	- в одну сторону	- fadnu storanu
- return	- туда и обратно	- tydah i abratna
- first class	- СВ	- es veh (SV)
What time does it leave/arrive?	В котором часу он отправляется/прибывает?	fkatoram chasu on atpravlyayetsa/pribyvayet?

Underground galleries

Moscow's metro stations are like underground galleries that display beautifully ornate works of Socialist Realism, such as huge chandeliers and magical mosaics.

Getting Around

Could you tell me when to get off?	Вы не подскажете когда мне выходить?	vy nye padskazhetye kagda mnye vykhodit?

Taxis

Unofficial taxis are generally bad news and should be avoided, unless you're prepared for a mystery tour, courtesy of a maverick chauffeur. Only use a respected cab company that a trustworthy Russian has recommended, agree the price before you get in and refuse to travel if the car looks unsafe. You can always get out.

I'd like a taxi to...	Мне такси до...	mnye taksi da...
How much is it to the...	Сколько будет стоить до...	skolka budyet stoyit da...
- airport?	- аэропорта?	- eraporta?
- town centre?	- центра города?	- tsentr gorada?
- hotel?	- гостиницы?	- gastinitsy?

Tours

In Russia's tourist hotspots there's no shortage of companies and individuals offering all kinds of walking tours, boat trips, hiking holidays, thematic excursions and jeep safaris. River cruises are popular in the capital, while Siberia offers unlimited opportunities to escape from civilisation on a trekking tour.

Are there any organised tours of the town/region?	Здесь есть экскурсии по городу/региону?	zdyes yest ekskursiyi pa goradu/regyonu?
Where do they leave from?	Откуда они отправляются?	atkuda ani atpravlyayutsa?
What time does it start?	Во сколько начало?	va skolka nachala?
Do you have English-speaking guides?	У вас есть англо-язычные гиды?	y vas yest anglo-yazichniye gidy?
Is lunch/tea included?	Это включая обед/ужин?	eta fkluchaya abyed/uzhin?
Do we get any free time?	У нас будет свободное время?	u nas budyet svabodnaye vremya?
Are we going to see...?	Мы увидим...?	my uvidim...?
What time do we get back?	Во сколько мы вернёмся?	va skolka my vyernyomsya?

Accommodation

Never before has Russia offered a greater assortment of places to lay your head, from luxurious 5-star Moscow hotels to basic lakeside camps. Booking from home is easy, with many hotels now featuring on-line reservation facilities, and travel agents listing countless options. Always make sure you have written confirmation before setting off.

On arrival, reception staff will briefly borrow your passport to register your visa. The receptionist, or *dezhurnaya*, will issue your key and payment is often made in advance.

Types of accommodation

The only accommodation options lacking in Russia are campsites, which are very rare, but wild camping by rivers and lakes is common. Big-city hotels come in two flavours – old Soviet dinosaurs and glitzy newbuilds. Backpacker hostels, homestays, holiday camps, spas and station dorms fill the gaps in between.

I'd like to stay in...	Я бы хотел (-ла) остановится в...	ya by khatyel (-la) astana<u>vits</u>a f...
- an apartment	- квартире	- kvar<u>tir</u>ye
- a campsite	- турбазе	- tur<u>ba</u>zye
- a hotel	- гостинице	- gas<u>tin</u>itsye
- a serviced room	- комнате с обслуживанием	- <u>kom</u>natye s obs<u>luzhi</u>vanyem
- a youth hostel	- хостеле	- <u>khos</u>telye
- a guest house	- в частном доме	- <u>fchas</u>tnam <u>dom</u>ye

Is it...	Это...	eta...
- full board?	- полный пансион?	- <u>pol</u>ny pan<u>sion</u>?
- half board?	- полупансион?	- palupan<u>sion</u>?
- self-catering?	- с самообслуж- иванием?	- sama'ab<u>sluzhi</u>- vanyem?

Home from home
Many Russians open up their houses to guests. These homestays can cost as little as R200 (£4) a night. Look out for the "Сдаются комнаты" (rooms for rent) sign.

Reservations

Do you have any rooms available?	У вас есть свободные номера?	u vas yest sva<u>bod</u>niye nom<u>era</u>?
Can you recommend anywhere else?	Где ещё вы бы порекомендо- вали?	gdye ye<u>sho</u> vy by porekomendo<u>va</u>li?
I'd like to make a reservation for...	Я бы хотел (-ла) забронировать на...	ya by kha<u>tyel</u> (-la) zabra<u>nir</u>ovach na...

- tonight	**- сегодня**	- sivodnya
- one night	**- одну ночь**	- ad<u>nu</u> noch
- two nights	**- две ночи**	- dvye <u>nochi</u>
- a week	**- неделю**	- nye<u>dye</u>lyu

From... (1st May)	**С...(первого мая)...**	s...(<u>pyer</u>vava <u>ma</u>ya)...
to... (8th May)	**по (восьмое мая)**	po (vas<u>mo</u>ye <u>ma</u>ya)

The lady of the landing
A throwback to Soviet times which still persists is the *dezhurnaya* or floor lady. Her job is to issue kcys and keep order. Our advice? Don't mess.

Room types

The most common room type is the twin with two single beds that can be pushed together. There are normally a number of singles and multi-room suites to choose from, too. Rooms can be en suite or have shared facilities, and all tend to have a TV and perhaps a fridge.

Do you have... room?	**У вас есть... номер?**	U vas yest... <u>no</u>mer
- a single	**- одноместный**	- adna<u>myest</u>ny
- a double	**- двухместный**	- dvukh<u>myest</u>ny
- a family	**- семейный**	- sem<u>yey</u>ny

with...	**с...**	s...
- a cot?	**- детской кроваткой?**	- <u>dyets</u>kay kra<u>vat</u>kay?
- twin beds?	**- отдельными кроватями?**	- at<u>dyel</u>nymi kra<u>vat</u>yami?
- a double bed?	**- двухспальной кроватью?**	- dvukh<u>spal</u>nay kra<u>vat</u>yu?
- a bath/shower?	**- ванной/душем?**	- <u>va</u>nay/<u>du</u>shem?
- air conditioning?	**- кондиционером?**	- konditsio<u>nye</u>rom?
- Internet access?	**- Интернетом**	- inter<u>ne</u>tom

Can I see the room?	**Можно посмотреть номер?**	<u>mozh</u>na pasmat<u>ret</u> <u>no</u>mer?

Prices

Room rates have shot up in recent years but still represent relatively good value for money. However, little extras such as phoning home, forays into the mini-bar or just borrowing an iron come with an extortionate price tag. Breakfast is also very often considered an extra, and many hotels do not offer it at all.

How much is...	Сколько стоит...	_skolka stoyit..._
- a double room?	- двухместный номер?	- _dvukhmyestny nomer?_
- per night?	- за ночь?	- _zanoch?_
- per week?	- за неделю?	- _za nyedyelyu?_
Is breakfast included?	Завтрак входит в цену?	_zaftrak fkhodit v tsenu?_
Do you have...	Вы делаете...	_vy dyelayetye..._
- a reduction for children?	- скидки для детей?	- _skidku dlya dyetyey?_
- a single room supplement?	- наценку на одноместный номер?	- _natsenka na adnamyestny nomer?_
Is there...	Здесь есть...	_zdyes yest..._
- a swimming pool?	- бассейн?	- _baseyn?_
- a lift?	- лифт?	- _lift?_
I'll take it	Я это возьму	_ya eta vazmu_
Can I pay by...	Можно заплатить...	_mozhna zaplatit..._
- credit card?	- кредитной карточкой?	- _kreditnay kartachkoy?_
- traveller's cheque?	- дорожными чеками?	- _darozhnymi chekami?_

Full steam ahead!

The _banya_, the Russian equivalent of the sauna, sees (mainly male) bathers whipping themselves with birch twigs (_venik_) in the heat before plunging into a cold pool.

All change!
Railway station resting rooms are dorms for passengers waiting for connections. Most are of a decent standard and boast good facilities. Rates are charged per hour.

Special requests

Could you...	Не могли бы вы...	nye magli by vy...
- put this in the hotel safe?	- положить это в сейф?	- palazhich-ts eta fseyf?
- order a taxi for me?	- заказать такси?	- zakazat taksi?
- wake me up at 7am?	- разбудить меня в (семь утра)?	- razbudich-ts menya f (sem utra)?
Can I have...	Я бы хотел (-ла)...	ya by khatyel (-la)...
- a room with a sea view?	- комнату с видом на море	- komnatu svidam na morye
- a bigger room?	- более просторный номер	- bolye prastorny nomer
- a quieter room?	- номер потише	nomer patisheh
Is there...	У вас есть...	u vas yest...
- a safe?	- сейф?	- seyf?
- a babysitting service?	- няни?	- nyani?
- a laundry service?	- прачечная?	- prachechnaya?
Is there wheelchair access?	Здесь можно проехать на инвалидной коляске?	zdyes mozhna prayekhat na invalidnam kalyaskye?

Checking in & out

I have a reservation for tonight	У меня бронь на сегодня	u menya bron na sivodnya
In the name of...	На имя...	na imya...

Here's my passport	Вот мой паспорт	vot moy _paspart_
What time is check out?	Когда я должен выселиться?	_kagda_ ya _dolzhen_ _vyselitsa_?
Can I have a later check out?	Могу я выселиться позже?	_magu_ ya vy_selitsa_ _pozhe_?
Can I leave my bags here?	Можно я оставлю свой багаж здесь?	_mozhna_ ya o_stavlyu_ svoy ba_gazh_ zdyes?
I'd like to check out	Я буду выселяться	ya _budu_ vysye_lyatsa_
Can I have the bill?	Счёт, пажалуйста	shchot, pa_zha_luysta

Camping

Do you have...	У вас есть...	u vas yest...
- a site available?	- свободное место?	- sva_bod_naye _myes_ta?
- electricity?	- электричество?	- elek_tri_chestva?
- hot showers?	- душ с горячей водой?	- dush sga_rya_chey va_doy_
- tents for hire?	- палатки напрокат?	- pa_lat_ka napra_kat_

How much is it per...	Сколько стоит за...	_skol_ka _sto_yit za...
- tent?	- палатку?	- pa_lat_ku?
- caravan?	- фургон?	- fur_gon_?
- person?	- человека?	- chela_vye_ka?
- car?	- машину?	- ma_shi_nu?

Where is/are the...	Где находится...	gdye na_kho_ditsa...
- reception?	- администратор	- adiminis_tra_tor?
- bathrooms?	- санузел?	- _sanu_zel?
- laundry facilities	- прачечная?	- _pra_chechnaya?

Yurt camps
Those holidaying in Eastern Siberia might consider a *yurt*, a circular felt tent used by nomads across the Central Asian steppe. They're surprisingly cosy, even when the mercury heads south.

Survival Guide

Although banks and ATMs can be found on every city street, small towns may only have one of each. Wi-Fi is spreading like digital wildfire through major cities, and internet cafés are ubiquitous. Even small villages have a post office, though postcards hardly ever beat their senders to the UK. Mobile phone roaming charges are astronomical, so if you're staying more than a few days, insert a local SIM card.

Travellers with disabilities will find Russia a challenge, but things in Moscow have improved slightly, with upmarket hotels catering for wheelchair users with specially designed rooms.

Money & banks

Where is the nearest...	Где находится ближайший...	gdye nakhoditsa blizhayshy...
- bank?	- банк?	- bank?
- ATM?	- банкомат?	- bankamat?
- foreign exchange office?	- пункт обмена валют?	- punkt abmyena valyut?

I'd like to...	Я бы хотел (-ла)...	ya by khatyel (-la)...
- withdraw money	- снять деньги со счёта	- snyat dyengi sashchota
- cash a traveller's cheque	- обналичить дорожные чеки	- abnalichit darozhnye cheki
- change money	- обменять деньги	- abmenyat dyengi
- arrange a transfer	- сделать денежный перевод	- sdyelach-ts dyenyezhny perevod

Could I have smaller notes, please?	Дайте, пожалуйста, более мелкие купюры	daytye, pazhaluysta, bolye myelkiye kupyury
What's the exchange rate?	Какой курс валюты?	kakoy kurs valyuty?
What's the commission?	Какой процент за обмен?	kakoy pratsent za abmyen?

What's the charge for...	Сколько стоит...	skolka stoyit...
- making a withdrawal?	- снять деньги?	- snyat dyengi?
- exchanging money?	- обменять валюту?	- abmenyach-ts valyutu?
- cashing a cheque?	- обналичить чек?	- abnalichit chek?

State of exchange?

Few Russian banks will exchange British pounds for roubles, so buy dollars or euros (or roubles) before you leave. Notes must be pristine, otherwise banks and exchange offices will refuse them.

What's the minimum/ maximum amount?	**Какая максимальная/ минимальная сумма?**	*kakaya maksimalnaya/ minimalnaya suma?*
This is not right	**Это неправильно**	*eta nyepravilna*
Is there a problem with my account?	**У меня проблема со счётом?**	*U menya prablyema sashchotam?*
The ATM took my card	**Банкомат забрал мою карточку**	*bankamat zabral mayu kartochku*
I've forgotten my PIN	**Я забыл свой код**	*ya zabyl svoy kod*

Post office

Where is the (main) post office?	**Где находится почта (главпочтампт)?**	*gdye nakhoditsa pochta (glavpochtamt)?*
I'd like to send a...	**Я хотел (-ла) бы отослать ...**	*ya khatyel (-la) by ataslat...*
- letter	**- письмо**	*- pismo*
- postcard	**- открытку**	*- atkrytku*
- parcel	**- посылку**	*- pasylku*
- fax	**- факс**	*- faks*
I'd like to send this...	**Я бы хотел (-ла) отослать это в...**	*ya by khatyel (-la) ataslat eta f...*
- to the United Kingdom	**- Великобританию**	*- velikabritaniyu*
- by airmail	**- авиапочтой**	*- aviapochtay*
- by express mail	**- экспресс-почтой**	*- ekspres-pochtay*
- by registered mail	**- заказным письмом**	*- zakaznym pismom*
I'd like...	**Я бы хотел (-ла)...**	*ya by khatyel (-la)...*
- a stamp for this letter/postcard	**- марку для этого письма/этой открытки**	*- marku dlya etava pisma/etay otkrytki*
- to buy envelopes	**- купить конверты**	*- kupit kanvyerty*
- to make a photocopy	**- сделать ксерокопию**	*- sdyelat kserokopiyu*
It contains...	**Это содержит...**	*eta sadyerzhit...*
It's fragile	**Это бьющееся**	*eta byushcheyesya*

Moscow calling
To call the UK from a Russian landline telephone, first dial 8, wait for a second ringtone, then key in 10, the country code (0044), then the subscriber number.

Telecoms

Where can I make an international phone call?	**Где можно позвонить за границу?**	gdye _mozhna_ pazva_nit_ zagra_ni_tsu?
Where can I buy a phone card?	**Где можно купить телефонную карточку?**	gdye _mozhna_ ku_pit_ tyele_fo_nuyu _kar_tochku?
How do I call abroad?	**Как звонить за границу?**	kak zva_nit_ zagra_ni_tsu?
How much does it cost per minute?	**Сколько это стоит в минуту?**	_skol_ka _eta_ _sto_yit v _mi_nutu?
The number is...	**Номер...**	_no_mer
What's the area/ country code for...?	**Какой код (города/ страны)...?**	ka_koy_ kod (_go_rada/ stra_ny_)...?
The number is engaged	**Занято**	_za_nyata
The connection is bad	**Плохая связь**	pla_kha_ya svyaz
I've been cut off	**Связь прервалась**	svyaz prer_va_las
I'd like...	**Дайте, пожалуйста...**	_day_tye pa_zha_luysta
- a charger for my mobile phone	**- зарядное устройство для моего мобильного телефона**	- zaryad_no_ye us_troy_stva dlya maye_vo_ ma_bil_nava tyele_fo_na
- an adaptor plug	**- переходник (адаптор) для розетки**	- perekhad_nik_ dlya ra_zyet_ki
- a pre-paid SIM card	**- проплаченную СИМ-карту**	- pra_pla_chenuyu SIM-_kar_tu

Internet

| Where's the nearest Internet café? | Где находится ближайшее интернет-кафе? | gdye nakhoditsa blizhaysheye internet kafeh? |
| Can I access the Internet here? | Здесь есть доступ к Интернету? | zdyes yest dostup k internetu? |

I'd like to...	Я бы хотел (-ла)...	ya by khatyel (-la)...
- use the Internet	- воспользоваться Интернетом	- vaspolzavatsa internetam
- check my email	- проверить электронную почту	- pravyerit elektronuyu pochtu
- use a printer	- воспользоваться принтером	- vaspolzavatsa printeram

How much is it...	Сколько стоит...	skolka stoyit...
- per minute?	- за минуту?	- za minutu?
- per hour?	- в час?	- fchas?
- to buy a CD?	- компакт-диск (DVD-диск)?	- kampakt-disk (DVD-disk)?

How do I...	Как мне...	kak mnye...
- log on?	- залогиниться?	- zalaginitsa?
- open a browser?	- зайти на страницу?	- zayti na stranitsu?
- print this?	- распечатать это?	- raspechatach-ts eta?

I need help with this computer	Мне нужна помощь возле этого компьютера	mnye nuzhna pomash vozlye etava kampyutera
The computer has crashed	Компьютер завис	kampyuter zavis
I've finished	Я закончил (-ла)	ya zakonchil (-la)

Chemist

| Where's the nearest (all-night) pharmacy? | Где находится ближайшая (круглосуточная) аптека? | gdye nakhoditsa blizhayshaya (kruglasutochnaya) aptyeka? |
| What time does the pharmacy open/close? | Во сколько аптека открывается/ закрывается? | va skolka aptyeka atkryvayetsa/ zakryvayetsa? |

I need something for...	Мне нужно что-нибудь от...	Mnye *nuzhna* shto-ni*but* at...
- diarrhoea	- поноса	- pa*nosa*
- a cold	- простуды	- pra*study*
- a cough	- кашля	- *kash*lya
- insect bites	- укусов насекомых	- u*ku*sav nase*ko*mykh
- sunburn	- солнечного ожога	- *sol*nyechnava a*zhoga*
- motion sickness	- укачивания	- u*ka*chivaniya
- hay fever	- сенной лихорадки	- senoy likha*rad*ki
- period pain	- менструальных болей	- menstru*al*nykh *bol*yey
- abdominal pains	- болей в животе	- *bol*yey vzhivo*tye*
- a urine infection	- цистита	- tsis*ti*ta
- a vaginal infection	- вагинита	- va*gi*nita
I'd like...	Мне нужен...	mnye *nuzhen*...
- aspirin	- аспирин	- aspi*rin*
- plasters	- пластырь	- *plas*tyr
- condoms	- презервативы	- prezer*va*tivy
- insect repellent	- защита от насекомых	- za*shchi*ta at nase*ko*mykh
- painkillers	- обезболивающее	- abez*ba*livayushiye
- a contraceptive	- противозача-точные	- prativaza*cha*-tachniye
How much should I take?	Как это принимать?	kak *eta* pri*nimat*?
Take...	Принимайте...	prini*may*tye...
- a tablet	- по одной таблетке	- pa ad*noy* tab*let*kye
- a teaspoon	- по чайной ложке	- pa *chay*noy *lozh*keh
- with water	- запивая водой	- zapi*vaya* va*doy*
How often should I take this?	Как часто это нужно принимать?	kak *chas*ta *eta* *nuzh*na prini*mat*?
- once/twice a day	- один раз/два раза в день	- a*din* raz/dva *ra*za vdyen
- before/after meals	- до/после еды	- do/*pos*lye *yedy*
- in the morning/ evening	- утром/вечером	- *ut*ram/*vye*cheram

Is it suitable for children?	Это можно детям?	eta *mozhna* *dyetyam?*
Will it make me drowsy?	Это не вызовет сонливость?	eta nye *vyzovyet* sonlivost?
Do I need a prescription?	Для этого нужен рецепт?	dlya *etava* *nuzhen* retsept?
I have a prescription	У меня есть рецепт	u *menya* yest retsept

Children

Where should I take the children?	Куда вы порекомендуете повести детей?	*kuda* vy parekamenduyetye pavesti dyetyey?
Where is...	Где находится...	gdye nakhoditsa...
- the nearest playground?	- ближайшая детская площадка?	- blizhayshaya detskaya plashchadka?
- the nearest fairground?	- ближайшие атракционы?	- blizhayshiye atraktsyony?
- the nearest zoo?	- зоопарк?	- za'apark?
- the nearest park?	- ближайший парк?	- blizhayshy park?
- the nearest swimming pool?	- ближайший бассейн?	- blizhayshy baseyn?
Is this suitable for children?	Это подходит для детей?	eta padkhodit dlya dyetyey?
Are children allowed?	Детям вход разрешён?	dyetyam fkhod razreshon?
Are there baby-changing facilities here?	здесь есть место для смены пелёнок?	zdyes yest myesta dlya smyeny pyelyonak?
Do you have...	У вас есть...	u vas yest...
- a children's menu?	- меню для детей?	- menyu dlya dyetyey?
- a high chair?	- высокий стульчик?	- vysoky stulchik?

Animal welfare

With kiddies in tow, a visit to the zoo may seem like a good idea. Make sure the zoo you are visiting treats its animals properly.

Is there...	Здесь есть...	zdyes yest...
- a child-minding service?	- няни?	- *nyani*?
- a nursery?	- детский сад?	- *dyetsky sad*?

Can you recommend a reliable babysitter?	Порекомендуйте надёжную няню	parekamen*duy*tye nad*yozh*nuyu *nyanyu*
Are the children constantly supervised?	Там дети под постоянным присмотром?	tam *dyeti* pad pasta*yan*ym pris*mo*tram?
When can I bring them?	Когда я могу их привести?	kagda ya ma*gu* yikh prive*sti*?
What time do I have to pick them up?	Во сколько их нужно забрать?	va *skolka* yikh *nuzh*na za*brat*?
He/she is... years old	Ему/ей ... лет/года	ye*mu*/yey... lyet/*go*da

I'd like to buy...	Я бы хотел (-ла) купить...	ya by kha*tyel* (-la) ku*pit*...
- nappies	- подгузники	- pad*guz*niki
- baby wipes	- гигиенические салфетки для детей	- gigiye*ni*cheskiye sal*fyet*ki dlya dye*tyey*
- tissues	- салфетки	- sal*fyet*ki

Travellers with disabilities

I have a disability	Я инвалид	ya inva*lid*
I need assistance	Мне нужна помощь	mnye *nuzh*na *po*mash
I am deaf	Я глухой	ya glukhoy
I have a hearing aid	У меня слуховой аппарат	u me*nya* slukha*voy* apa*rat*
I can't walk well	Мне трудно ходить	mnye *trud*na kha*dit*
Is there a lift?	Здесь есть лифт?	zdyes yest lift?
Is there wheelchair access?	Здесь можно проехать на инвалидной коляске?	zdyes *mozh*na pra*ye*khat na inva*lid*nay kal*ya*skye?
Can I bring my guide dog?	Можно я с собой приведу собаку-гида?	*mozh*na ya sa*boy* prive*du* ca*ba*ku-*gi*da?

Are there disabled toilets?	Здесь есть туалеты для инвалидов?	zdyes yest tualyety dlya invalidaf?
Do you offer disabled assistance?	Вы оказываете услуги для инвалидов?	vy akazyvayetye uslugi dlya invalidaf?
Could you help me...	Вы мне не поможете...	vy mnye nye pamozhetye...
- cross the street?	- перейти улицу?	- pereyti ulitsu?
- go up/down the stairs?	- подняться/ спуститься по лестнице?	- padnyatsa/ spustitsa pa lestnitse?
Can I sit down somewhere?	Можно я где-нибудь присяду?	mozhna ya gdye-nibut prisyadu?
Could you call an accessible taxi for me?	Вы бы не могли вызвать такси для инвалидов?	vy by nye magli vyzvat taksi dlya invalidaf?

Repairs & cleaning

This is broken	Это поломано	eta palomana
Can you fix it?	Вы можете это починить?	vy mozhetye eta pachinit?
Do you have...	У вас есть...	u vas yest...
- a battery?	- батарейка?	- batareyka?
- spare parts?	- запчасти?	- zapchasti?
Can you... this?	Вы можете это...	vy mozhetye eta...
- clean	- почистить?	- pachistit?
- press	- отутюжить?	- atutyuzhit?
- dry-clean	- почистить?	- pachistit?
- patch	- заштопать?	- zashtopat?
When will it be ready?	Когда это будет готово?	kagda eta budyet gatova?
This isn't mine	Это не моё	eta nye mayo

Tourist information

| Where's the Tourist Information Office? | Где находится информацион-ный центр? | gdye nakhoditsa informatsyony tsentr? |
| Do you have a city/ regional map? | У вас есть карта города/региона? | u vas yest karta gorada/regyona? |

What are the main places of interest?	Какие места самые интересные?	kakiye myesta samiye intyeresniye?
Could you show me on the map?	Покажите мне это на карте?	pakazhitye mnye eta na kartye?
We'll be here for...	Мы тут будем...	my tut budyem...
- half a day	- полдня	- poldnya
- a day	- день	- dyen
- a week	- неделю	- nyedyelyu
Do you have a brochure in English?	У вас есть брошюры на английском?	u vas yest brashury na angliyskom?
We're interested in...	Нас интересует...	nas interesuyet...
- history	- история	- istoriya
- architecture	- архитектура	- arkhitektura
- shopping	- магазины	- magaziny
- hiking	- пеший туризм	- pyeshy turizm
- a scenic walk	- прогулки на природе	- pragulki na prirodye
- a boat cruise	- прогулки на катере	- pragulki na katyerye
- a guided tour	- экскурсии с гидом	- ekskursiyi s gidam
Are there any excursions?	У вас есть экскурсии?	u vas yest ekskursiyi?
How long does it take?	Сколько это занимает времени?	skolka eta zanimayet vremeni?
What does it cost?	Сколько это стоит?	skolka eta stoyit?
What days is it open/closed?	По каким дням это открыто/закрыто?	pa kakym dnyam eta atkryta/zakryta?
What time does it open/close?	Во сколько это открывается/закрывается?	va skolka eta atkryvayetsa/zakryvayetsa?
What's the admission price?	Сколько стоит входной билет?	skolka stoyit fkhadnoy bilyet?
Are there any tours in English?	У вас есть туры на английском?	u vas yest tury na angliyskom?

Emergencies

Russia is not a dangerous place. Take the same precautions to stay safe that you do back home, and you'll be fine.

Emergency medical treatment in state-run hospitals is free for UK citizens, though facilities are of a poor standard. Moscow has several private Western-standard clinics that charge hefty sums for treatment. Make sure all of your vaccinations are up to date before leaving, in particular Hepatitis A and B. A jab protecting against tick-born encephalitis is also advisable for outdoor activities. Comprehensive travel insurance is a must for anyone travelling to Russia. Make sure your policy actually covers Russia, as well as any activities you plan to do there.

Medical

Where is...	Где находится...	gdye nakhoditsa...
- the hospital?	- больница?	- balnitsa?
- the health centre?	- поликлиника?	- paliklinika?
I need...	Мне...	mnye...
- a doctor	- нужен врач	- nuzhen vrach
- a female doctor	- нужна женщина-врач	- nuzhna zhenshchina-vrach
- an ambulance	- нужна скорая помощь	- nuzhna skoraya pomashch
It's very urgent	Это очень срочно	eta ochen srochna
I'm injured	У меня ранение	u menya ranyeniye
Can I see a doctor?	Я хочу видеть врача	ya khachu videt vracha
I don't feel well	Я плохо себя чувствую	ya plokha sebya chustvuyu
I have...	У меня...	u menya...
- a cold	- простуда	- prastudah
- diarrhoea	- понос	- panos
- a rash	- сыпь	- syp
- a temperature	- температура	- temperaturah
I have a lump here	У меня здесь опухоль	u menya zdyes opukhal
It hurts here	У меня болит здесь	u menya balit zdyes
It hurts a lot/ a little	Болит сильно/ несильно	balit silna/ nyesilna
How much do I owe you?	Сколько я вам должен?	skolka ya vam dolzhen?
I have insurance	У меня есть страховка	u menya yest strakhovka

Dentist

I need a dentist	Мне нужен зубной врач	mnye nuzhen zubnoy vrach
I have tooth ache	У меня болит зуб	u menya balit zub
My gums are swollen	У меня воспалены дёсны	u menya vaspalyeny dyosny
This filling has fallen out	У меня выпала пломба	u menya vypala plomba
I have an abscess	У меня абсцесс	u menya abses
I have broken a tooth	У меня отвалился кусок зуба	u menya atvalilsa kusok zuba
Are you going to take it out?	Вы собираетесь его вырывать?	vy sabirayetyes yevo vyryvat?

| Can you fix it temporarily? | **Вы можете поставить временную пломбу?** | *vy mozhetye pastavit vremenuyu plombu?* |

Emergency numbers
In an emergency, call the following numbers free of charge from any phone: Fire: 01; Police: 02; Ambulance: 03; Moscow English-language emergency number: 937 9999

Crime

I want to report a theft	**Я хочу сообщить о краже**	*ya khachu sa'abshchit a krazheh*
Someone has stolen my...	**у меня украли...**	*u menya ukrali...*
- bag	**- сумку**	*- sumku*
- car	**- машину**	*- mashinu*
- credit cards	**- кредитные карточки**	*- kreditniye kartochki*
- money	**- деньги**	*- dyengi*
- passport	**- паспорт**	*- paspart*
I've been attacked	**На меня напали**	*na menya napali*

Lost property

I've lost my...	**Я потрерял (-ла)...**	*ya patyeryal (-la)...*
- car keys	**- ключи от машины**	*- klyuchi at mashiny*
- driving licence	**- водительское удостоверение**	*- vadityelskoye udastovyeryenye*
- handbag	**- сумку**	*- sumku*
- flight tickets	**- билеты на самолёт**	*- bilyety na samalyot*
It happened...	**Это случилось...**	*eta sluchilos...*
- this morning	**- сегодня утром**	*- sivodnya utram*
- today	**- сегодня**	*- sivodnya*

| - in the hotel | - в гостинице | - fgastinitsye |
| I left it in the taxi | Я забыл (-ла) это в такси | ya zabyl (-la) eta ftaksi |

Breakdown

I've had...	У меня...	u menya...
- an accident	- произошла авария	- praizashla avariya
- a breakdown	- произошла поломка	- praizashla palomka
- a puncture	- прокололась шина	- prakalolas shina
My battery is flat	У меня сел аккумулятор	u menya syel akumulyatar
I don't have a spare tyre	У меня нет запасного колеса	u menya nyet zapasnova kalesa
I've run out of petrol	У меня закончился бензин	u menya zakonchilsa benzin
My car won't start	Моя машина не заводится	maya mashina nye zavoditsa
Can you repair it?	Вы сможете это починить?	vy smozhetye eta pachinit?
How long will it take?	Сколько на это уйдёт времени?	skolka na eta uydyot vremyeni?
I have breakdown cover	У меня есть страховка на случай поломки	u menya yest strakhovka na sluchay palomki

Problems with the authorities

I'm sorry, I didn't realise...	Извините, я не знал что...	izvinitye, ya nye znal shto...
- I was driving so fast	- я ехал так быстро	- ya yekhal tak bystra
- I went over the red lights	- я проехал на красный свет	- ya prayekhal na krasny svyet
- it was against the law	- это запрещено	- eta zapreshcheno
Here are my documents	Вот мои документы	vot mayi dakumyenty
I'm innocent	Я невиновен (-на)	ya nyevinovyen (-na)

professor
фе́ссор.
profit ['profit] 1) 2)при-
вы́года; по́льза; 2) *v* 1) прино-
быль; 2. *v* 1) прино-
си́ть по́льзу; 2) извле-
ка́ть по́льзу; **~able**
[-əbl] 1) прибы́льный;
вы́годный; поле́зный;
profound [prə'faund]
глубо́кий;
program(me) ['prou-
græm] програ́мма.
programming ['prou-
græmiŋ] программи́-
рова́ние.
progress 1. *n* ['prougres]
продвиже́ние; раз-
ви́тие, прогре́сс; 2.
v [prə'gres] продви-
га́ться; де́лать успе́хи
~ive [prə'gresiv] 1)
прогресси́вный, пере-
дово́й; 2) возраста́ю-

действова...
promotion [..
1) повыше́ние; 2) соде́й...
же́ние;
вие.
prompt [prompt] немедлен-
бы́стрый; 2. *v* 1) побужда́ть;
ный; 2. *v* 1) подска́зывать;
да́ть; 2) ['prompts] су-
~er ['prompts]
флёр.
pronoun ['prounaun]
грам. местоиме́ние.
pronounce [prə'nauns]
произноси́ть.
pronunciation [prənʌn-
si'eiʃn] произноше́ние.

Dictionary

This section consists of two parts:
an English-Russian dictionary to
help you get your point across and a
Russian-English section to decipher
the reply. Even if you find yourself
reading directly from this book,
syllable by syllable, enhancing your
performance with an element of mime,
the locals will be mightily impressed by
the fact that you are making an effort.

Just a reminder on pronunciation:
stress is very important and can change
the meaning of the word according to
where it falls. We have underlined the
syllable that must be clearly emphasised,
with all others rising to, or falling away
from, it. Note that the letter "ё" is
always stressed.

English-Russian dictionary

A

A&E	Скорая помощь	*skoraya pomash*
about (concerning)	о	*oh*
accident	авария	*avariya*
accommodation	жильё	*zhilyo*
aeroplane	самолёт	*samalyot*
again	опять	*apyat*
ago	тому назад	*tamu nazad*
AIDS	СПИД	*speed*
airmail	авиапочта	*aviapochta*

airport	**аэропорт**	***aeraport***

Moscow has five airports. Most international flights
land at Sheremetevo 2 and Domodedovo.

alarm	тревога	*trevoga*
all	всё	*vsyo*
all right	хорошо	*kharashoh*
allergy	аллергия	*alergiya*
ambulance	машина скорой помощи	*mashina skoroy pomoshchi*
America	Америка	*amerika*
American	американец	*amerikanyets*
and	и	*ih*
anniversary	годовщина	*gadavshchina*
another	другой	*drugoy*
to answer	ответить	*atvyetit*
any	любой	*lyuboy*
apartment	квартира	*kvartira*
appointment	встреча	*vstrecha*
April	апрель	*aprel*
area	район	*rayon*
area code	код города	*kod gorada*
around	вокруг	*vakrug*
to arrange	договориться	*dagavaritsa*
arrival	прибытие	*pribitiye*
art	искусство	*iskustva*
to ask	спрашивать	*sprashivat*
aspirin	аспирин	*aspirin*
at (time)	в	*v*
August	август	*avgust*
Australia	Австралия	*avstraliya*
Australian	австралиец	*avstraliyets*
available	есть в наличии	*yest vnalichiyi*
away	в отъезде	*vat'yezdye*

B

baby	ребёнок	ribyonok
back (body)	спина	spina
back (place)	сзади	szadyi
bad	плохой	plakhoy
baggage	багаж	bagazh
bar (pub)	бар (паб)	bar (pab)
bath	ванна	vanah
to be	быть	bit
beach	пляж	plyazh
because	потому что	patamu shta
because of	из-за	iz-za
best	лучший	luchshy
better	лучше	luchsheh
between	между	mezhdu
bicycle	велосипед	velasiped
big	большой	balshoy
bill	счёт	shchyot
bit (a)	немного	nyemnoga
boarding card	посадочный талон	pasadachny talon
book	книга	kniga
to book	бронировать	braniravat
booking	бронирование	braniravaniye
box office	касса	kasa
boy	мальчик	malchik
brother	брат	brat
bureau de change	пункт обмена валют	punkt abmyena valyut
to burn	жечь	zhech
bus	автобус	avtobus
business	бизнес	biznes
but	но	noh
to buy	купить	kupit
by (air, car, etc)	на	nah
by (beside)	у	u
by (via)	через	cherez

C

café	кафе	kafeh
to call	звонить	zvanit
camera	фотоаппарат	fot 'aparat
can (to be able)	мочь	moch
to cancel	отменить	atmyenit
car	машина	mashina
carnival	карнавал	carnaval
cash	наличные деньги	nalichniye dyengi
cash point	банкомат	bankamat
casino	казино	kazinoh
castle	замок	zamak
cathedral	собор	sabor

CD	компакт-диск	*kompakt' disk*
centre	центр	*tsentr*
to change	менять	*menyat*
charge	цена	*tsena*
to charge	запросить	*zaprasit*
cheap	дешёвый	*dyeshovy*
to check in (hotel)	вселиться (в гостиницу)	*fselitsa (fgastinitsu)*
to check in (airport)	регистрироваться (в аэропорту)	*registrirovatsa (v aerapartu)*
cheque	чек	*chek*
child	ребёнок	*ribyonok*
to choose	выбрать	*vybrat*
cigar	сигара	*sigara*
cigarette	сигарета	*sigaretah*
cinema	кинотеатр	*kinoteatr*
city	город	*gorad*
to close	закрыть	*zakrit*
close by	недалеко	*nyedaleko*
closed	закрытый	*zakrity*

clothes	**одежда**	***adyezhda***

Temperatures across Russia seldom rise above freezing in winter. Packing warm clothes is a must.

club	клуб	*klub*
coast	побережье	*poberezhiye*
coffee house	кафе	*kafeh*
cold	холодно	*kholadna*
colour	цвет	*tsvyet*
to complain	жаловаться	*zhalavatsa*
complaint	жалоба	*zhalaba*
to confirm	подтвердить	*pat'tverdit*
confirmation	подтверждение	*pat'tverzhdyeniye*
consulate	консульство	*konsulstva*
to contact	связаться	*svyazatsa*
contagious	заразный	*zarazny*
cool	прохладный	*prakhladny*
cost	цена	*tsena*
to cost	стоить	*stoyit*
cot	детская кроватка	*dyetskaya kravatka*
country	страна	*strana*
countryside	природа	*priroda*
cream	сливки	*slivky*
credit card	кредитная карточка	*kreditnaya kartochkah*
crime	преступление	*prestuplyeniye*

currency	валюта	*valyuta*

The Russian currency is the rouble, which is divided into 100 kopecks.

customer	клиент	*kliyent*
customs	таможня	*tamozhnya*
cut	разрез	*razrez*
to cut	резать	*rezat*
cycling	езда на велосипеде	*yezdah na velasipedye*

D

damage	урон	*uron*
danger	опасность	*apasnost*
daughter	дочь	*doch*
day	день	*dyen*
December	декабрь	*dyekabr*
to dehydrate	обезвоживать	*abezvozhivat*
delay	задержка	*zadyerzhka*
to dial	набирать	*nabirat*
difficult	трудный	*trudny*
directions	направление	*napravlyeniye*
dirty	грязный	*gryazny*
disabled	инвалид	*invalid*
discount	скидка	*skidka*
district	район	*rayon*
to disturb	беспокоить	*bespakoyit*
doctor	врач	*vrach*
double	двойной	*dvaynoy*
down	вниз	*vniz*
to drive	вести	*vesti*
driver	водитель	*vaditel*
driving licence	водительское удостоверение	*vaditelskoye udastavereniye*
drug	лекарство	*lekarstva*
to dry-clean	чистить в химчистке	*chistich-ts fkhimchistkye*
dry-cleaner's	химчистка	*khimchistka*
during	во время	*va vremya*
duty (tax)	налог	*nalog*

E

early	рано	*rana*
e-mail	электронная почта	*elektronaya pochta*
embassy	посольство	*pasolstva*
emergency	крайняя необходимость	*kraynyaya nyeabkhadimast*
England	Англия	*angliya*

English   английский   *angliysky*

Outside of Moscow and St Petersburg, few waiters, receptionists and tour guides speak English.

enough	достаточно	*dastatachna*
entrance	вход	*fkhod*
error	ошибка	*ashybka*
exactly	точно	*tochna*
exchange rate	курс обмена валют	*kurs abmyena valyut*
exhibition	выставка	*vystavka*
exit	выход	*vykhad*
express (delivery)	срочная доставка	*srochnaya dastavka*
express (train)	экспресс (поезд)	*ekspres (poyezd)*

F

facilities	условия	*usloviya*
far	далеко	*daleko*
father	дальше	*dalsheh*
favourite	любимый	*lyubimy*
February	февраль	*fevral*
festival	фестиваль	*festival*
filling station	автозаправка	*avtozapravka*
film (camera)	фотоплёнка	*fotaplyonka*
film (cinema)	кинофильм	*kinafilm*
fire	пожар	*pazhar*
fire exit	пожарный выход	*pazharny vykhad*
first aid	первая помощь	*pyervaya pomash*
fitting room	примерочная	*primyerachnaya*

flight   полёт   *palyot*

The safety record of the Russian national airline Aeroflot has improved immensely in recent years.

flu	грипп	*grip*
food poisoning	пищевое отравление	*pishchevoye atravlyeniye*
football	футбол	*futbol*
for	для	*dlya*
form (document)	анкета	*ankyeta*
free	свободный	*svabodny*
free (money)	бесплатный	*besplatny*
friend	друг	*drug*
from	с, из	*s, iz*

G

gallery	галерея	*galereya*
garage	гараж	*garazh*

gas	**газ**	*gaz*
gents (toilets)	**мужской туалет**	*muzh<u>skoy</u> tua<u>let</u>*
girl	**девочка, девушка**	*<u>dye</u>vachka, <u>dye</u>vushka*
glasses	**очки**	*ach<u>ki</u>*
golf	**гольф**	*golf*
golf course	**поле для игры в гольф**	*<u>po</u>lye dlya <u>ig</u>ry vgolf*
good	**хороший**	*kha<u>rosh</u>y*
group	**группа**	*<u>gru</u>pa*
guarantee	**гарантия**	*ga<u>ran</u>tiya*
guide	**гид**	*gid*

H

hair	**волосы**	*<u>vo</u>lasy*
hairdresser's	**парикмахерская**	*parik<u>ma</u>kerskaya*
half	**половина**	*pala<u>vi</u>na*
heat	**жара**	*zha<u>ra</u>*
help!	**помогите!**	*pama<u>gi</u>tye!*
here	**здесь**	*zdyes*
high	**высокий**	*vy<u>so</u>ky*
holiday (work-free day)	**выходной**	*vykhad<u>noy</u>*
holidays	**отпуск**	*<u>ot</u>pusk*

homosexual	**гомосексуалист**	*homosexua<u>list</u>*

Russia is still conservative about homosexuality. Displays
of same-sex affection are generally frowned upon.

hospital	**больница**	*bal<u>ni</u>tsa*
hot	**горячий**	*gar<u>ya</u>chy*
how?	**как?**	*kak?*
how big?	**какой размер?**	*ka<u>koy</u> raz<u>myer</u>?*
how far?	**как далеко?**	*kak dale<u>ko</u>?*
how long?	**как долго?**	*kak <u>dol</u>ga?*
how much?	**сколько?**	*<u>skol</u>ka?*
hurry up!	**поторопитесь!**	*patara<u>pi</u>tyes!*
husband	**муж**	*muzh*

I

identity card	**удостоверение личности**	*udastavye<u>re</u>niye <u>lich</u>nasti*
ill	**больной**	*bal<u>noy</u>*
immediately	**немедленно**	*ne<u>med</u>lena*
important	**важный**	*<u>vazh</u>ny*
in	**в**	*f, v*
information	**информация**	*infar<u>mat</u>siya*
inside	**внутри**	*vnu<u>tri</u>*

insurance	страховка	*strakhovka*

Make sure your insurance policy actually covers
Russia and any activities you plan to do there.

interesting	интересный	*interesny*
international	международный	*mezhdunarodny*
Ireland	Ирландия	*irlandiya*
Irish	ирландский	*irlandsky*
island	остров	*ostrav*
itinerary	маршрут	*marshrut*

J

January	январь	*yanvar*
jet ski	водные лыжи	*vodniye lyzhi*
journey	путешествие	*puteshestviye*
July	июль	*iyul*
junction	перекрёсток	*perekryostak*
June	июнь	*iyun*
just (only)	только	*tolka*

K

key	ключ	*klyuch*
key ring	брелок	*bryelok*
keyboard	клавиатура	*klaviatura*
kid	ребёнок	*rebyonak*
kind (person)	добрый	*dobry*
kind (sort)	сорт	*sort*
kiosk	киоск	*kiosk*

kiss	поцелуй	*patseluy*

Kiss Russian women on both cheeks after an initial
meeting. Don't try this with men.

L

label	марка, ярлык	*marka, yarlyk*
ladies (toilets)	женский туалет	*zhensky tualyet*
lady	женщина	*zhenshchina*
lake	озеро	*ozera*
language	язык	*yazyk*
last	последний	*pasledny*
late (delayed)	с опозданием	*sapazdaniyem*
late (time)	поздний	*pozdny*
launderette	прачечная	*prachechnaya*
lawyer	юрист	*yurist*
less	меньше	*mensheh*
library	библиотека	*bibliateka*
life jacket	спасательный жилет	*spasatelny zhilet*

lifeguard	спасатель	spasatyel
lift	лифт	lift
like	как	kak
little	немного	nemnoga
local	местный	mestny
to lose	терять	teryat
lost property	утерянные вещи	uteryanie veshchi
luggage	багаж	bagazh

M

madam	госпожа	gaspazha
mail	почта	pochta
main	главный	glavny
man	мужчина	mushchina
manager	менеджер	menedzher
many	много	mnoga
map (city)	карта города	karta gorada
map (road)	карта	karta
March	март	mart
market	базар	bazar
married	женат	zhenat
May	май	may
maybe	может быть	mozhet bit
mechanic	механический	mekhanichesky
meeting	встреча	vstrecha
message	сообщение	sa'abshcheniye
midday	полдень	polden
midnight	полночь	polnach
minimum	минимум	minimum
minute	минута	minuta
missing	недостающий	nedastayushy
mobile phone	мобильный телефон	mabilny tyelefon
moment	момент	mament
money	деньги	dengi
more	больше	bolsheh
mosquito	комар	kamar
most	большинство	balshinstvo
mother	мама	mamah
much	много	mnoga
museum	музей	muzey
musical	музыкальный	muzikalny
must	должен	dolzhen
my	мой	moy

N

name	имя	imya
nationality	национальность	natsionalnost
near	возле	vozlye
necessary	необходимый	neabkhadimy

never	никогда	*nikagda*
new	новый	*novy*
news	новости	*novasti*

newspaper газета *gazyeta*
The English-language *Moscow Times* is widely
available from newsstands and upmarket hotels.

next	следующий	*sleduyushchy*
next to	рядом с	*ryadam s*
nice	приятный	*priyatny*
nice (people)	приятные (люди)	*priyatniye (lyudi)*
night	ночь	*noch*
nightclub	ночной клуб	*nachnoy klub*
north	север	*sever*
note (money)	денежная банкнота/ купюра	*denezhnaya banknota/ kupyurah*
nothing	ничего	*nichevo*
November	ноябрь	*nayabr*
now	сейчас	*seychas*
nowhere	нигде, никуда	*nigdye, nikudah*
nudist beach	нудистский пляж	*nudistky plyazh*
number (figure)	номер	*nomer*
number (of items)	число	*chislo*

O

object	предмет	*predmet*
October	октябрь	*aktyabr*
off (switched)	выключить	*vyklyuchit*
office	офис	*ofis*
ok	хорошо	*kharashoh*
on	на	*nah*
once	один раз	*adin raz*
only	только	*tolka*
open	открыто	*atkryta*
to open	открыть	*atkryt*
operator	телефонист	*telefonist*
opposite (place)	напротив	*naprotiv*
optician's	магазин оптики	*magazin optiki*
or	или	*ili*
other	другой	*drugoy*
out of order	неисправный	*neispravny*
outdoor	на природе	*na prirode*
outside	на улице	*na ulitseh*
overnight	ночной	*nachnoy*
owner	владелец	*vladelets*
oxygen	кислород	*kislarod*

P

painkiller	**обезболивающие**	*abezbalivayushiye*
pair	**пара**	*para*
parents	**родители**	*raditeli*
park	**парк**	*park*
parking	**парковка**	*parkovka*
party	**вечеринка**	*vecherinka*

passport	**паспорт**	***paspart***

Carry your passport with you at all times. You'll need it for travelling, hotels and as a means of ID.

people	**люди**	*lyudi*
perhaps	**возможно**	*vazmozhna*
person	**человек**	*chelavek*
petrol	**бензин**	*benzin*
photo	**фотография**	*fotagrafiya*
phrase book	**разговорник**	*razgavornik*
place	**место**	*mesta*
platform	**платформа**	*platforma*
police	**милиция**	*militsiya*
port (sea)	**порт**	*port*
possible	**возможно**	*vazmozhna*
post	**почта**	*pochta*
post office	**почта**	*pochta*
prescription	**рецепт**	*retsept*
price	**цена**	*tsena*
private	**частный**	*chastny*
probably	**возможно**	*vazmozhna*
problem	**проблема**	*prablema*
pub	**паб**	*pab*
public transport	**общественный транспорт**	*abshestveny transpart*

Q

quality	**качество**	*kachestva*
quantity	**количество**	*kalichestva*
query	**осведомляться**	*asvedamlyatsa*
question	**вопрос**	*vapros*

queue	**очередь**	***ochered***

Russian queues can be a harrowing experience for Brits, with many people pushing in.

quick	**быстрый**	*bystry*
quickly	**быстро**	*bystra*
quiet	**тихий**	*tikhy*

quite	вполне	*fpalnye*
quiz	викторина	*viktarina*

R

radio	радио	*radio*
railway	железная дорога	*zheleznaya daroga*
rain	дождь	*dozhd*
rape	изнасилование	*iznasilavaniye*
ready	готовый	*gatovy*
real	настоящий	*nastayashchy*
receipt (written)	квитанция	*kvitantsiya*
receipt (printed)	чек	*chek*
reception	администрация	*administratsiya*
receptionist	администратор	*administratar*
reduction	снижение	*snizheniye*
refund	возврат денег	*vazvrat deneg*
region	регион	*region*
to relax	расслабляться	*raslablyatsa*
rent	арендная плата	*arendnaya plata*
to rent	снимать	*snimat*
reservation	резервирование	*rezerviravaniye*

retired	**на пенсии**	**na pensiyi**

Don't expect any concessions on public transport
or at museums if you're over 65 years of age.
Reduced rates are rare.

rich	богатый	*bagaty*
road	дорога	*daroga*
room	комната	*komnata*
route	маршрут	*marshrut*
rude	грубый	*gruby*
ruins	развалины	*razvaliny*
to run	бежать	*bezhat*

S

safe	безопасный	*bezapasny*
sauna	сауна	*sauna*
Scotland	Шотландия	*shatlandiya*
Scottish	шотландский	*shatlandsky*
sea	море	*morye*
seat	место	*mesta*
seat belt	ремень безопасности	*remen bezapasnasti*
sedative	успокоительное средство	*uspokoyitelnoye sredstva*
see you later!	до встречи!	*da fstrechi!*
self-service	самообслуживание	*sama'absluzhivaniye*

September	сентябрь	sentyabr
service	обслуживание	absluzhivaniye
shop	магазин	magazin
shopping	делать покупки	delat pakupki
shopping centre	торговый центр	targovy tsentr
short	короткий	karotky
to show	показывать	pakazyvat
shut	закрывать	zakryvat
sign	знак	znak
signature	подпись	podpis
since	с	s
sir	сэр	ser
sister	сестра	sestra
ski	лыжи	lyzhi
sleeping pill	снотворная таблетка	snatvornaya tablyetka
slow	медленно	myedlena
small	маленький	malenki
soft	мягкий	myahki
some	немного	nyemnoga
something	что-то	shtota
son	сын	syn
soon	скоро	skora
south	юг	yug
South Africa	Южно-Африканская Республика	yuzhna-afrikanskaya respublika
South African	южно-африканский	yuzhna-afrikansky
speed	скорость	skorast

| sport | спорт | sport |

Russia has won the ice hockey World Championship an amazing 24 times.

stadium	стадион	stadyon
staff	штат	shtat
stamp	марка	marka
station	станция	stantsiya
sterling pound	фунт стерлингов	funt sterlingaf
straight	прямой	pryamoy
street	улица	ulitsa
stress	стресс	stres
suitcase	чемодан	chemadan
sun	солнце	sontseh
sunglasses	очки	achki
surname	фамилия	familiya
swimming pool	бассейн	baseyn
switched on	включён	fkluchon
symptom	симптом	simptom

T

table	**стол**	stol
to take	**взять**	vzyat
tampons	**тампоны**	tampony
tax	**налог**	nalog
tax free	**без налога**	bez naloga
taxi	**такси**	taksi
telephone	**телефон**	tyelefon
telephone box	**таксофон**	taksafon
television	**телевизор**	tyelevizar
tennis	**теннис**	tenis
tennis court	**теннисный корт**	tenisny kort
to text	**посылать SMS**	pasylat SMS
that	**тот**	tot
theft	**кража**	krazha
then	**потом**	patom
there	**там**	tam
thing	**вещь**	vyeshch
to think	**думать**	dumat
thirsty (I am)	**я хочу пить**	ya khachu pit
this	**этот**	etat
through	**через**	cherez
ticket (bus)	**билет на автобус**	bilyet na avtobus
ticket (cinema)	**билет в кино**	bilyet fkino
ticket (parking)	**талон на парковку**	talon na parkovku
ticket office	**касса**	kasa

time	**время**	vremya

Russia stretches across ten time zones! When it's midday in Moscow, it's bedtime in Petropavlovsk-Kamchatsky.

timetable	**расписание**	raspisaniye
tip (money)	**чаевые**	chayeviye
tired	**уставший**	ustavshy
to	**к**	k
to (the left/right)	**налево/направо**	nalyeva/naprava
today	**сегодня**	sivodnya
toilet	**туалет**	tualyet
toiletries	**косметические принадлежности**	kasmeticheskiye prinadlezhnasti
toll	**пошлина**	poshlina
tomorrow	**завтра**	zaftra
tonight	**сегодня вечером**	sivodnya vyecheram
too	**тоже**	tozhe

tourist office	туристический инфоцентр	*turistichestky infatsentr*

Beware any organisation claiming to be a Russian state-funded tourist information centre. There is no such thing.

town	город	*gorad*
town hall	городская администрация	*garadskaya administratsiya*
train	поезд	*poyezd*
tram	трамвай	*tramvay*
to translate	переводить	*perevadit*
to travel	путешествовать	*putyeshestvavat*
travel agency	турагенство	*turagenstva*
true (right)	правдивый	*pravdivy*
typical	типичный	*tipichny*

U

ulcer	язва	*yazva*
umbrella	зонтик	*zontik*
uncomfortable	неудобный	*nyeudobny*
unconscious	без сознания	*bez saznaniya*
under	под	*pod*

underground	метро	*metro*

Moscow and St Petersburg are currently the only cities in Russia with an underground railway system.

to understand	понять	*panyat*
underwear	нижнее бельё	*nizhnyeye byelyo*
unemployed	безработный	*bezrabotny*
unpleasant	неприятный	*nyepriyatny*
up	наверх	*navyerkh*
upstairs	наверху	*navyerkhu*
urgent	срочно	*srochna*
to use	пользоваться	*polzavatsa*
useful	полезный	*palyezny*
usually	обычно	*abychna*

V

vacant	свободный	*svabodny*
vacation	каникулы	*kanikuly*
vaccination	прививка	*privivka*
valid	действительный	*dyeystvityelny*

valuables	ценные вещи	_tsen'niye_ _vyeshchi_
value	цена	_tsenah_
VAT	подоходный налог	_padakhodny nalog_
vegetarian	вегетарианский	_vegetariansky_
vehicle	транспортное средство	_transpartnaye sredstva_
very	очень	_ochen_

visa	**виза**	_**viza**_

You must register your visa within three days of arrival in the country.

visit	посещение	_paseshcheniye_
to visit	посещать	_paseshchat_
vitamin	витамин	_vitamin_
to vomit	рвать	_rvat_

W

waiter/waitress	официант/ официантка	_ofitsiant/ ofitsiantka_
waiting room (station)	комната ожидания	_komnata azhidaniya_
Wales	Уэльс	_uels_
to walk	идти	_iti_
wallet	бумажник	_bumazhnik_
to want	хотеть	_khatyet_
to wash	стирать	_stirat_
watch	часы	_chasy_
water	вода	_vadah_
water sports	водные виды спорта	_vodnye vidy sporta_
way (manner)	манера	_manyera_
way (route)	маршрут	_marshrut_
way in	вход	_fkhod_
way out	выход	_vykhad_
weather	погода	_pagoda_
web	сеть	_set_

website	**вебсайт**	_**vebsayt**_

Russia's website suffix is ".ru", but many sites also use ".com"

week	неделя	_nyedyelya_
weekday	рабочий день	_rabochy dyen_
weekend	выходные	_vykhadniye_
welcome	добро пожаловать	_dabro pazhalavach_
well	хорошо	_kharashoh_
Welsh	валлийский	_valiysky_
west	запад	_zapad_

what?	что?	*shto?*
wheelchair	инвалидное кресло	*invalidnaye kresla*
when?	когда?	*kagda?*
where?	где?	*gdye?*
which?	который?	*katory?*
while	во время	*vavremya*
who?	кто?	*kto?*
why?	почему?	*pachemu?*
wife	жена	*zhena*
wine	вино	*vino*
with	с	*s*
without	без	*bez*
woman	женщина	*zhenshina*
wonderful	чудесный	*chudyesny*
word	слово	*slova*
work	работа	*rabota*
to work	работать	*rabotat*
world	мир	*mir*
worried	переживающий	*perezhivayushy*
to write	писать	*pisat*
wrong (mistaken)	неправильный	*nyepravilny*

X

x-ray	рентген	*rengen*
to x-ray	сделать рентген	*sdyelat rengen*

Y

yacht	яхта	*yakhta*
year	год	*god*
yearly	ежегодно	*yezhegodna*
yellow pages	жёлтые страницы	*zholtye stranitsy*
yes	да	*dah*
yesterday	вчера	*fchera*
yet	ещё	*yesho*
you (formal)	Вы	*vy*
you (informal)	ты	*ty*
young	молодой	*maladoy*
your (formal)	ваш	*vash*
your (informal)	твой	*tvoy*
youth hostel	общежитие	*obshezhitiye*

Z

zebra crossing	пешеходный переход	*peshekhodny perekhod*
zero	ноль	*nol*
zone	зона	*zona*
zoo	зоопарк	*za'apark*

Russian-English dictionary

А

август	_avgust_	August
австралиец	_avstraliyec_	Australian
Австралия	_avstraliya_	Australia
автобус	_avtobus_	bus
автозаправка	_avtozapravka_	filling station
администратор	_administratar_	receptionist
администрация	_administratsiya_	reception
английский	_angliysky_	English
Англия	_angliya_	England
анкета	_ankyeta_	form (document)
апрель	_aprel_	April
арендная плата	_arendnaya plata_	rent
аспирин	_aspirin_	aspirin

Б

багаж	_bagazh_	baggage, luggage
базар	_bazar_	market

банкомат	**_bankamat_**	**cash point**

There are now ATMs in every town and city across the Russian Federation.

бар (паб)	_bar (pab)_	bar (pub)
бассейн	_baseyn_	swimming pool
бежать	_byezhat_	to run
без	_bez_	without
без налога	_bez naloga_	tax free
безопасный	_bezapasny_	safe
безработный	_bezrabotny_	unemployed
без сознания	_bez saznaniya_	unconscious
бензин	_benzin_	petrol
бесплатный	_besplatny_	free (money)
беспокоить	_bespakoyit_	to disturb
библиотека	_bibliatyeka_	library
бизнес	_biznes_	business
билет в кино	_bilyet fkino_	ticket (cinema)
билет на автобус	_bilyet na avtobus_	ticket (bus)
богатый	_bagaty_	rich
больница	_balnitsa_	hospital
больной	_balnoy_	ill
больше	_bolsheh_	more
большинство	_balshenstvo_	most
большой	_balshoy_	big
брат	_brat_	brother
брелок	_bryelok_	key ring
бронирование	_bronirovaniye_	reservation

бронировать *bronirovat* **to book**
Book a visit to Moscow's famous Bolshoy Ballet, a lifetime cultural highlight.

бумажник	*bumazhnik*	wallet
быстро	*bystra*	quickly
быстрый	*bystry*	quick
быть	*bit*	to be

B

в	*f, v*	at (time); in
важный	*vazhny*	important
валлийский	*valiysky*	Welsh
валюта	*valyuta*	currency
ванна	*vanah*	bath
ваш	*vash*	your (formal)
вебсайт	*vebsayt*	website

вегетарианский *vegetariansky* **vegetarian**
Vegetarians are best advised to try the drool-worthy choices offered by Georgian eateries.

велосипед	*velasiped*	bicycle
вести	*vesti*	to drive
вечеринка	*vyecherinka*	party
вещь	*vyeshch*	thing
взять	*vzyat*	to take
виза	*viza*	visa
викторина	*viktarina*	quiz
вино	*vino*	wine
витамин	*vitamin*	vitamin
включён	*fkluchon*	switched on
владелец	*vladyelets*	owner
вниз	*vniz*	down
внутри	*vnutri*	inside
во время	*va vremya*	during; while
вода	*vadah*	water
водитель	*vaditel*	driver
водительское удостоверение	*vaditelskoye udastavyeryeniye*	driving licence
водные виды спорта	*vodnye vidy sporta*	water sports
водные лыжи	*vodniye lyzhi*	jet ski
возврат денег	*vazvrat dyeneg*	refund
возле	*vozlye*	near
возможно	*vazmozhna*	perhaps; possible; probably
вокруг	*vakrug*	around
волосы	*volasy*	hair

вопрос	vapros	question
в отъезде	vat'yezdye	away
вполне	fpalnye	quite
врач	vrach	doctor
время	vremya	time
вселиться	fselitsa	to check in (hotel)
(в гостиницу)	(fgastinitsu)	
встреча	vstrecha	meeting

вход	fkhod	entrance; way in

The tourist entrance to the symbol of state power, the Moscow Kremlin, is in Alexandrovsky Garden.

вчера	fchera	yesterday
Вы	vy	you (formal)
выбрать	vybrat	to choose
выключить	vyklyuchit	off (switched)
высокий	vysoky	high
выставка	vystavka	exhibition
выход	vykhad	exit; way out
выходной	vykhadnoy	holiday (work-free day)
выходные	vykhadniye	weekend

Г

| газ | gaz | gas |
| газета | gazyeta | newspaper |

галерея	galereya	gallery

Moscow's Tretyakov Gallery holds the world's greatest collection of Orthodox icons.

гараж	garazh	garage
гарантия	garantiya	guarantee
где?	gdye?	where?
гид	gid	guide
главный	glavny	main
год	god	year
гольф	golf	golf
гомосексуалист	homosexualist	homosexual
город	gorad	city; town
городская	garadskaya	town hall
администрация	administratsiya	
горячий	garyachy	hot
госпожа	gaspazha	madam
готовый	gatovy	ready
грипп	grip	flu
грубый	gruby	rude
группа	grupa	group

грязный	*gryazny*	dirty

Д

да	*dah*	yes
далеко	*daleko*	far
дальше	*dalsheh*	father
двойной	*dvaynoy*	double
девочка, девушка	*dyevachka, dyevushka*	girl
действительный	*dyeystvityelny*	valid
декабрь	*dyekabr*	December
делать покупки	*dyelat pakupki*	shopping
денежная банкнота/ купюра	*dyenezhnaya banknota/ kupyurah*	note (money)
день	*dyen*	day
деньги	*dyengi*	money
детская кроватка	*dyctckaya kravatka*	cot
дешёвый	*dyeshovy*	cheap
диск	*disk*	CD
для	*dlya*	for
до встречи!	*da fstrechi*	see you later!
добро пожаловать	*dabro pazhalavach*	welcome
добрый	*dobry*	kind (person)
договориться	*dagavaritsa*	to arrange
дождь	*dozhd*	rain
должен	*dolzhen*	must
дорога	*daroga*	road
достаточно	*dastatachna*	enough
дочь	*doch*	daughter
друг	*drug*	friend
другой	*drugoy*	other
думать	*dumach*	to think

Е

ежегодно	*yezhegodna*	yearly
езда на велосипеде	*yezda na velasipedye*	cycling
есть в наличии	*yest fnalichi*	available
ещё	*yesho*	yet

Ж

жалоба	*zhalaba*	complaint
жаловаться	*zhalavatsa*	to complain
жара	*zhara*	heat

железная дорога *zhelyeznaya daroga* **railway**
Russian Railways employ 1.2 million people and
administer over 60,000 miles of track.

жёлтые страницы	*zholtye stranitsy*	yellow pages
жена	*zhena*	wife
женат	*zhenat*	married

женский туалет *zhensky tualyet* ladies (toilets)
Public loos are rare in Russia, so if you need to "spend a kopeck", head for a restaurant or hotel.

| женщина | *zhenshina* | lady, woman |
| жечь | *zhech* | to burn |

З

завтра	*zaftra*	tomorrow
задержка	*zadyerzhka*	delay
закрывать	*zakryvat*	shut
закрытый	*zakrity*	closed
замок	*zamak*	castle
запад	*zapad*	west
запросить	*zaprasit*	to charge
заразный	*zarazny*	contagious

звонить *zvanit* to call
Phone boxes have a "таксофон" sign. All take phone cards, which can be bought at newsstands and kiosks.

здесь	*zdyes*	here
знак	*znak*	sign
зона	*zona*	zone
зонтик	*zontik*	umbrella

зоопарк *za'apark* zoo
Moscow Zoo offers one of the few opportunities you'll ever have of seeing a real Siberian tiger.

И

идти	*iti*	to walk
из	*iz*	from
из-за	*iz-za*	because of
изнасилование	*iznasilavaniye*	rape
или	*ili*	or
имя	*imya*	name
инвалид	*invalid*	disabled
инвалидное кресло	*invalidnaye kresla*	wheelchair
интересный	*intyeresny*	interesting
информация	*infarmatsiya*	information
Ирландия	*irlandiya*	Ireland

ирландский	*irlandsky*	Irish
искусство	*iskustva*	art
июль	*iyul*	July
июнь	*iyun*	June

К

к	*k*	to
казино	*kazinoh*	casino
как	*kak*	like
как?	*kak?*	how?
как далеко?	*kak daleko?*	how far?
как долго?	*kak dolga?*	how long?
какой размер?	*kakoy razmyer?*	how big?

| **каникулы** | ***kanikuly*** | **vacation** |

During the long summer holidays, Russian cities empty, with everyone heading off into the countryside.

карнавал	*carnaval*	carnival
карта	*karta*	map (road)
карта города	*karta gorada*	map (city)
касса	*kasa*	box office; ticket office
кафе	*kafeh*	café; coffee house
качество	*kachestva*	quality
квитанция	*kvitantsiya*	receipt
кинотеатр	*kinoteatr*	cinema
кинофильм	*kinafilm*	film (cinema)
киоск	*kiosk*	kiosk
кислород	*kislarod*	oxygen
клавиатура	*klaviatura*	keyboard
клиент	*kliyent*	customer
клуб	*klub*	club
ключ	*klyuch*	key
книга	*kniga*	book
когда?	*kagda?*	when?
код города	*kod gorada*	area code
количество	*kalichestva*	quantity

| **комар** | ***kamar*** | **mosquito** |

Mosquitoes can be a real summer pest across Russia, even in Moscow.

комната	*komnata*	room
комната ожидания	*komnata azhidaniya*	waiting room (station)
консульство	*konsulstva*	consulate
короткий	*karotky*	short

косметические принадлежности	*kasmeticheskiye prenadlezhnasti*	toiletries
который?	*katory?*	which?
кража	*krazha*	theft
крайняя необходимость	*kraynyaya nyeabkhadimast*	emergency
кредитная карточка	*kreditnaya kartochkah*	credit card
кто?	*kto?*	who?
купить	*kupit*	to buy
курс обмена валют	*kurs abmyena valyut*	exchange rate

Л

лекарство	*lekarstva*	drug
лифт	*lift*	lift
лучше	*luche*	better
лучший	*luchshy*	best
лыжи	*lyzhi*	ski
любимый	*lyubimy*	favourite
люди	*lyudi*	people

М

| магазин | *magazin* | shop |
| магазин оптики | *magazin optiki* | optician's |

| май | *may* | May |

For Moscow's May 1st parade, the entire city centre goes into lock-down for the whole day.

маленький	*malenki*	small
мальчик	*malchik*	boy
мама	*mama*	mother
манера	*manyera*	way (manner)
марка	*marka*	label; stamp
март	*mart*	March
маршрут	*marshrut*	itinerary; route; way (route)
машина	*mashina*	car
медленно	*myedlena*	slow
между	*mezhdu*	between
международный	*mezhdunarodny*	international
менеджер	*menedzher*	manager
меньше	*mensheh*	less
менять	*menyat*	to change
местный	*myestny*	local
место	*myesta*	place; seat
метро	*metro*	underground (tube)
механический	*mekhanichesky*	mechanic

милиция	*militsiya*	police
минимум	*minimum*	minimum
минута	*minuta*	minute
мир	*mir*	world
много	*mnoga*	many; much
мобильный телефон	*mabilny tyelefon*	mobile phone
может быть	*mozhet bit*	maybe
мой	*moy*	my
молодой	*maladoy*	young
момент	*mamyent*	moment
море	*morye*	sea
мочь	*moch*	can (to be able)
муж	*muzh*	husband
мужской туалет	*muzhskoy tualyet*	gents (toilets)
мужчина	*mushchina*	man

| музей | *muzey* | museum |

Charging foreigners a higher admission charge than Russians at tourist attractions is an unfortunate hangover from Soviet times.

| музыкальный | *muzikalny* | musical |
| мягкий | *myahki* | soft |

Н

на	*nah*	by (air, car, etc); on
набирать	*nabirat*	to dial
наверх	*navyerkh*	up

| наверху | *navyerkhu* | upstairs |

In Russia, the first floor is the ground floor. This can often be confusing in lifts.

налево/направо	*nalyeva/naprava*	to (the left/right)
наличные деньги	*nalichniye dyengi*	cash
налог	*nalog*	duty (tax), tax
на пенсии	*na pensiyi*	retired
направление	*napravlyeniye*	directions
на природе	*na prirodye*	outdoor
напротив	*naprotiv*	opposite (place)
настоящий	*nastayashchy*	real
на улице	*na ulitsye*	outside
национальность	*natsionalnost*	nationality
недалеко	*nyedaleko*	close by
неделя	*nyedyelya*	week
недостающий	*nyedastayushy*	missing
неисправный	*nyeispravny*	out of order

немедленно	nye*myed*lena	immediately
немного	nyem*noga*	bit (a); little; some
необходимый	nyeabkha*dimy*	necessary
неправильный	nye*pra*vilny	wrong (mistaken)
неприятный	nyepri*yat*ny	unpleasant
неудобный	nyu*dob*ny	uncomfortable
нигде	ni*gdye*	nowhere
нижнее бельё	*nizh*nyeye bye*lyo*	underwear
никогда	nika*gda*	never
ничего	niche*vo*	nothing
но	noh	but
новости	*no*vast	news
новый	*no*vy	new
ноль	nol	zero
номер	*no*mer	number (figure)
ночной	nach*noy*	overnight
ночной клуб	nach*noy* klub	nightclub
ночь	noch	night
ноябрь	na*yabr*	November
нудистский пляж	nu*distky* plyazh	nudist beach

O

обезболивающие	abez*ba*livayushiye	painkiller
обезвоживать	abez*vo*zhivat	to dehydrate
обслуживание	ab*slu*zhivaniye	service
общественный транспорт	ab*shest*veny *trans*part	public transport
обычно	a*bych*na	usually
одежда	ad*yezh*da	clothes
один раз	a*din* raz	once

| озеро | *o*zyera | lake |

Lake Baikal in Eastern Siberia is the world's deepest lake, holding a fifth of the planet's fresh water.

октябрь	ak*tyabr*	October
опасность	a*pas*nost	danger
осведомляться	asvyedam*lyat*sa	query

| остров | *o*strav | island |

St Petersburg was built on a series of islands in the delta formed by the River Neva.

| открыто | at*kry*ta | open |

24-hour food shops are now the norm in every town across Russia.

открыть	*atkryt*	to open
отменить	*atmyenich*	to cancel
отпуск	*otpusk*	holidays
офис	*ofis*	office
официант/	*ofitsiant/*	waiter/waitress
официантка	*ofitsiantka*	
очень	*ochen*	very
очередь	*ochered*	queue
очки	*achki*	glasses, sunglasses
ошибка	*ashybka*	error

П

паб	*pab*	pub
пара	*para*	pair
парикмахерская	*parikmakerskaya*	hairdresser's
парк	*park*	park
парковка	*parkovka*	parking
паспорт	*paspart*	passport
первая помощь	*pyervaya pomashch*	first aid
переводить	*perevadit*	to translate
переживающий	*perezhivayushy*	worried
перекрёсток	*perekryostak*	junction
пешеходный	*peshekhodny*	zebra crossing
переход	*perekhod*	
писать	*pisat*	to write
пищевое	*pishchevoye*	food poisoning
отравление	*atravlyeniye*	
платформа	*platforma*	platform
плохой	*plakhoy*	bad

| **пляж** | ***plyazh*** | **beach** |

The best place in Russia for a beach holiday is the Black Sea coast in the south.

побережье	*poberezhiye*	coast
погода	*pagoda*	weather
под	*pod*	under
подоходный налог	*padakhodny nalog*	VAT
подпись	*podpis*	signature
подтвердить	*potverdit*	to confirm
подтверждение	*potverzhdyeniye*	confirmation
поезд	*poyezd*	train
пожар	*pazhar*	fire
пожарный выход	*pazharny vykhad*	fire exit
поздний	*pozdny*	late (time)
показывать	*pakazyvach*	to show
полдень	*poldyen*	midday
поле для игры	*polye dlya*	golf course
в гольф	*igry fgolf*	

полезный	*palyezny*	useful
полёт	*palyot*	flight
полночь	*polnach*	midnight
половина	*palavina*	half
пользоваться	*polzavatsa*	to use
помогите!	*pamagitye!*	help!
понять	*panyat*	to understand
порт	*port*	port (sea)
посадочный талон	*pasadachny talon*	boarding card
посещать	*paseshchat*	to visit

посещение	*paseshcheniye*	visit

St Petersburg's Hermitage is a must-visit that houses over three million pieces of art.

последний	*paslyedny*	last
посольство	*pasolstva*	embassy
посылать SMS	*pasylat SMS*	to text
потом	*patom*	then
потому что	*patamushta*	because
поторопитесь!	*potarapityes!*	hurry up!
поцелуй	*patseluy*	kiss
почему?	*pachemu?*	why?
почта	*pochta*	mail; post; post office
пошлина	*poshlina*	toll
правдивый	*pravdivy*	true (right)
прачечная	*prachechnaya*	launderette
предмет	*predmyet*	object
преступление	*prestuplyeniye*	crime
прибытие	*pribitiye*	arrival
прививка	*privivka*	vaccination
примерочная	*primyerachnaya*	fitting room
природа	*priroda*	countryside
приятные (люди)	*priyatniye (lyudi)*	nice (people)
приятный	*priyatny*	nice
проблема	*prablyema*	problem
прохладный	*prakhladny*	cool
прямой	*pryamoy*	straight
пункт обмена валют	*punkt abmyena valyut*	bureau de change
путешествие	*puteshestviye*	journey
путешествовать	*putyeshestvavat*	to travel

Р

работа	*rabota*	work
работать	*rabotat*	to work (machine), to work (person)
рабочий день	*rabochy dyen*	weekday
радио	*radio*	radio
развалины	*razvaliny*	ruins

разговорник	*razgavornik*	phrase book
разрез	*razrez*	cut
район	*rayon*	area, district
рано	*rana*	early
расписание	*raspisaniye*	timetable
расслабляться	*raslablyatsa*	to relax
рвать	*rvat*	to vomit
ребёнок	*ribyonok*	baby, child, kid
регион	*regyon*	region
регистрироваться	*registrirovatsa*	to check in (airport)
(в аэропорту)	*(v erapartu)*	
резать	*rezat*	to cut
резервирование	*reservirovaniye*	booking, reservation
резервировать	*reserviravat*	to book
ремень	*remen*	seat belt
безопасности	*bezapasnosti*	
рентген	*rcngcn*	x ray
рецепт	*retsept*	prescription
родители	*raditeli*	parents
рядом с	*ryadam s*	next to

С

с	*s*	from, since, with
самообслуживание	*sama'absluzhivaniye*	self-service
сауна	*sauna (like 'ow'*	sauna
	in 'how')	
свободный	*svabodny*	free; vacant
связаться	*svyazatsa*	to contact
сделать рентген	*sdyelat rengen*	to x-ray
север	*syever*	north
сегодня	*sivodnya*	today
сегодня вечером	*sivodnya vyecheram*	tonight
сейчас	*seychas*	now
сентябрь	*sentyabr*	September
сестра	*sestra*	sister
сеть	*set*	web
сзади	*szadyi*	back (place)
сигара	*sigara*	cigar
сигарета	*sigareta*	cigarette
симптом	*simptom*	symptom
скидка	*skidka*	discount
сколько?	*skolka?*	how much?
скоро	*skora*	soon
скорость	*skorast*	speed
следующий	*slyeduyushchy*	next
сливки	*slivky*	cream
слово	*slova*	word
снижение	*snizheniye*	reduction
снимать	*snimat*	to rent

снотворная таблетка	snatvornaya tablyetka	sleeping pill
собор	sabor	cathedral
солнце	sontseh	sun
сообщение	sa'abshcheniye	message
с опозданием	sapazdaniyem	late (delayed)
сорт	sort	kind (sort)
спасатель	spasatyel	lifeguard
спасательный жилет	spasatyelny zhilyet	life jacket
спина	spina	back (body)
спорт	sport	sport
спрашивать	sprashivat	to ask
срочная доставка	srochnaya dastavka	express (delivery)
срочно	srochna	urgent
стадион	stadyon	stadium
станция	stantsiya	station
стирать	stirat	to wash
стоить	stoyit	to cost
стол	stol	table

страна	strana	country

Russia has land borders with a whopping 14 countries, from Norway to North Korea.

страховка	strakhovka	insurance
стресс	stres	stress
счёт	schyot	bill
сын	syn	son
сэр	ser	sir

Т

такси	taksi	taxi
таксофон	taksafon	telephone box
талон на парковку	talon na parkovku	ticket (parking)
там	tam	there
таможня	tamozhnya	customs
тампоны	tampony	tampons
твой	tvoy	your (informal)
телевизор	tyelevizar	television
телефон	tyelefon	telephone
телефонист	tyelefonist	operator
теннис	tenis	tennis
теннисный корт	tenisny kort	tennis court
терять	tyeryat	to lose
типичный	tipichny	typical
тихий	tikhy	quiet
тоже	tozhe	too
только	tolka	only
торговый центр	targovy tsentr	shopping centre

тот	tot	that
точно	tochna	exactly
трамвай	tramvay	tram
транспортное средство	transpartnaye sredstva	vehicle
трудный	trudny	difficult
туалет	tualyet	toilet
турагенство	turagenstva	travel agency
туристический инфоцентр	turistichestky infatsentr	tourist office
ты	ty	you (informal)

у

у	u	by (beside)
удостоверение личности	udastavyereniye lichnasti	identity card
улица	ulitsa	street
урон	uron	damage
условия	usloviya	facilities
успокоительное средство	uspokoyityelnoye sredstva	sedative
уставший	ustavshy	tired
утерянные вещи	utyeryaniye vyeshchi	lost property
Уэльс	uels	Wales

Ф

| фамилия | familiya | surname |

In between a Russian's first name and surname is their patronymic (a name derived from ancestors).

февраль	fevral	February
фестиваль	festival	festivals
фотоаппарат	fot 'aparat	camera
фотография	fotagrafiya	photo
фотоплёнка	fotaplyonka	film (camera)
фунт стерлингов	funt sterlingaf	sterling pound
футбол	futbol	football

х

химчистка	khimchistka	dry-cleaner's
холодно	kholadna	cold
хороший	kharoshy	good
хорошо	kharashoh	ok; well
хотеть	khatyet	to want

ц

| цвет | tsvyet | colour |
| цена | tsena | cost, price, value, charge |

| ценные вещи | *tseniye vyeshchi* | valuables |
| центр | *tsentr* | centre |

Ч

чаевые	*chayeviye*	tip (money)
частный	*chastny*	private
часы	*chasy*	watch
чек	*chek*	cheque, receipt (shopping)
человек	*chelavyek*	person
чемодан	*chemadan*	suitcase
через	*cherez*	by (via); through
число	*chislo*	number (of items)
чистить в химчистке	*chistit fkhimchistkye*	to dry-clean
что?	*shto?*	what?
что-то	*shto-ta*	something
чудесный	*chudyesny*	wonderful

Ш

Шотландия	*shatlandiya*	Scotland
шотландский	*shatlandsky*	Scottish
штат	*shtat*	staff

Э

экспресс (поезд)	*ekspres (poyezd)*	express (train)
электронная почта	*elektronaya pochta*	e-mail
этот	*etat*	this

Ю

юг	*yug*	south
Южно-Африканская Республика	*yuzhna-afrikanskaya respublika*	South Africa
южно-африканский	*yuzhna-afrikansky*	South African
юрист	*yurist*	lawyer

Я

| язва | *yazva* | ulcer |

| **язык** | ***yazyk*** | **language** |

The Russian language has virtually no distinct regional accents.

январь	*yanvar*	January
ярлык	*yarlyk*	label
я хочу пить	*ya khachu pit*	thirsty (I am)
яхта	*yakhta*	yacht

Quick reference

Numbers

0	**ноль**	*nol*
1	**один**	*adin*
2	**два**	*dva*
3	**три**	*tri*
4	**четыре**	*chetyri*
5	**пять**	*pyat*
6	**шесть**	*shest*
7	**семь**	*syem*
8	**восемь**	*vosem*
9	**девять**	*dyevyat*
10	**десять**	*dyesat*
11	**одиннадцать**	*adinatsat*
12	**двенадцать**	*dvyenatsat*
13	**тринадцать**	*trinatsat*
14	**четырнадцать**	*chetyrnatsat*
15	**пятнадцать**	*pyatnatsat*
16	**шестнадцать**	*shestnatsat*
17	**семнадцать**	*syemnatsat*
18	**восемнадцать**	*vasyemnatsat*
19	**девятнадцать**	*dyevyatnatsat*
20	**двадцать**	*dvatsat*
21	**двадцать один**	*dvatsat adin*
30	**тридцать**	*tritsat*
40	**сорок**	*sorak*
50	**пятьдесят**	*pyatdyesyat*
60	**шестьдесят**	*shestdyesyat*
70	**семьдесят**	*syemdyesyat*
80	**восемьдесят**	*vosyemdyesyat*
90	**девяносто**	*dyevyanosta*
100	**сто**	*sto*
1000	**тысяча**	*tysyacha*
1st	**первый**	*pyervy*
2nd	**второй**	*ftaroy*
3rd	**третий**	*tryety*
4th	**четвёртый**	*chetvyorty*
5th	**пятый**	*pyaty*

Weights & measures

gram (=0.03oz)	грамм	*gram*
kilogram (=2.2lb)	килограмм	*kilogram*
pound (=0.45kg)	фунт	*funt*
centimetre (=0.4in)	сантиметр	*santimetr*
metre (=1.1yd)	метр	*metr*
kilometre (=0.6m)	километр	*kilametr*
litre (=2.1pt)	литр	*litr*

Days & time

Monday	понедельник	*panyedyelnik*
Tuesday	вторник	*ftornik*
Wednesday	среда	*sreda*
Thursday	четверг	*chetverg*
Friday	пятница	*pyatnitsa*
Saturday	суббота	*subota*
Sunday	воскресенье	*vaskreseniye*

What time is it?	Который час?	*katory chas?*
(Four) o'clock	(Четыре) часа	*(chetyri) chasa*
Quarter past (six)	Четверть (седьмого)	*chetvert (syedmova)*
Half past (eight)	Пол (девятого)	*pol (dyevyatava)*
Quarter to (ten)	Без пятнадцати (десять)	*bez pyatnatsati (dyesyat)*
morning	утро	*utra*
afternoon	полдень	*poldyen*
evening	вечер	*vyecher*
night	ночь	*noch*

Clothes size conversions

Women's clothes	34	36	38	40	42	44	46	50
equiv. UK size	6	8	10	12	14	16	18	20

Men's jackets	44	46	48	50	52	54	56	58
equiv. UK size	34	36	38	40	42	44	46	48

Men's shirts	36	37	38	39	40	41	42	43
equiv. UK size	14	14.5	15	15.5	16	16.5	17	17.5

Shoes	36.5	37.5	39	40	41.5	42.5	44	45
equiv. UK size	4	5	6	7	8	9	10	11